MODER

BY THE SAME AUTHOR

Il Camino del Serpente
The Cosmic Influence
Encyclopedia of Fortune Telling
Magic: The Western Tradition
The Magical World of Aleister Crowley
The Rebirth of Magic (with Isabel Sutherland)
Rudolf Steiner and Holistic Medicine
Satan and Swastika
Tantra for Westerners
Techniques of High Magic (with Stephen Skinner)
Wisdom from Afar
Witchcraft and Demonology

EDITED BY THE SAME AUTHOR

Astral Projection, Ritual Magic and Alchemy (by S.L. MacGregor
    Mathers and Others)
The Grimoire of Armadel

MODERN RITUAL MAGIC

THE RISE OF WESTERN OCCULTISM

FRANCIS KING

PRISM · UNITY

Originally published as *Ritual Magic in England* in 1970 by Neville Spearman Limited

This revised edition published in Great Britain in 1989 by

PRISM PRESS
2 South Street
Bridport
Dorset DT6 3NQ

and distributed in the USA by

AVERY PUBLISHING GROUP INC.
350 Thorens Avenue
Garden City Park
New York 11040

and published in Australia 1989 by

UNITY PRESS
6a Ortona Road
Lindfield
NSW 2070

1 85327 032 6

Printed and bound in the Channel Islands
by The Guernsey Press Limited

CONTENTS

CONTENTS

ACKNOWLEDGMENTS

To Dr. F. I. Regardie for permission to quote a passage from his *Tree of Life*, recently reprinted by Samuel L. Weiser Inc. To Messrs. Hutchinson for permission to quote from the *Occult Review*; to Messrs. Thorson for permission to quote a passage from Dion Fortune's *Psychic Self Defence*; to the Britons Publishing Co. for permission to make quotations; to the kindness of Mr. John Symonds for stating that, as Crowley's literary executor, he had no objection to me quoting Crowley's original ideas for the ordeals of his new Magical Order; to Mr. D. Edwards and the Wardens of the Order of the Cubic Stone for permission to quote from *The Monolith*.

To G.A.D. for help at all stages of the writing of this book; to Christine Crystal for her assistance with the Index; to Stanley Waters for his assistance with typing; and, finally, a special thank you to Gerald Yorke for his kindness, loan of documents, and tremendous help—particularly in the early stages of my research.

FOREWORD

From time to time the English newspapers report the desecration of some deserted country Church for the purposes of 'Black Magic', or comment upon the activities of some minor cult or secret society. Frequently these stories are illustrated with the photographs of naked, or semi-naked, men and women engaged in either dancing around a blazing fire or standing rapt before a crude altar on which are displayed swords, scourges, oil, knives and the other traditional impedimenta of the sorcerer.

These newspaper reports are only the tip of the iceberg, an outward and rather exhibitionistic manifestation of the astonishing revival of mediaeval magic and alchemy that has taken place in the nineteenth and twentieth centuries.

This rebirth of interest in subjects which the nineteenth century agnostics thought of as having been swept into the dustbin of history is not only of interest to those concerned with occult studies in general, and ritual magic in particular, but, in fact, has far wider implications. For the story of how this revival occurred throws much light on the early lives and beliefs of such apparently diverse characters as W. B. Yeats, Aleister Crowley, and Charles Williams and is, at the same time, of a certain general sociological importance.

My real story begins in 1887, but, as the general reader might find it difficult to plunge into the events of that and following years without, at least, some knowledge of the survival of the magical-mystical tradition in Western Europe, I have thought it advisable to both outline the Rosicrucian legend and its ramifications in eighteenth and nineteenth century Europe and to give a brief account of the survival of magic in England. This I have done in my early chapters; such of my readers as are familiar with this material could, with advantage, skip these sections of the book and commence with the chapter entitled 'Dr. Westcott and a Goat'.

CHAPTER ONE

The Rosicrucian Legend

As was the case in the rest of Western Europe the religious life of mediaeval England was, to all appearances, orthodox and impeccably Catholic; from time to time, it is true, some wandering Franciscan friar would have to be burnt for teaching a neo-Joachimite heresy, and in the fifteenth century there was an epidemic of Lollardry—but these were comparatively unimportant.

Beneath this outward conformity, however, were concealed a substantial amount of magic, peasant superstition, neo-Gnostic cultism, and, if one chooses to accept the thesis of Dr. Margaret Murray (which I don't), the still living remains of the great fertility religion of Western Europe.

Magic, that is to say methods of entering into relationships with non-human forces and obtaining wealth, power, and pleasure, must have been studied and practiced by many seemingly orthodox and respectable individuals. This is clear from the considerable number of manuscripts of the grimoires—text books of ritual magic—that have survived to this day; there must have been many pious priests and laymen who kept a copy of *The Key of Solomon* or the *Great Grimoire* carefully concealed within their homes.

It might have been expected that such practices and beliefs would have become less commonplace during the Renaissance, that era of cultivated, rational, and urbane Priests who avoided reading their Missals for fear that the badness of the Latin might corrupt their style. On the contrary, however, interest in magic became more widespread than at any time since the latter days of the Roman Empire and the grimoires began to circulate in printed form; it is significant that Reginald Scot, the sixteenth century Kentish squire and author, had in his library copies of almost every grimoire of any importance.

At the beginning of the seventeenth century there were many mystics and magicians in England. Some were harmless; quiet country clergymen who studied the Christian Qabalah of Mirandola and the Neo-Platonists of Florence, others were more sinister. Dr. Lamb, for example, a confidant of the dissolute Duke of Buckingham, not only practiced the black arts but raped a little girl (in the process infecting her with a venereal disease) and was eventually murdered by an irate London mob, while Simon Forman not only practiced magic, divination, and astrology, but was an expert on poisons and was in some way involved in the notorious Somerset murder.

Whether 'black' or 'white' all these mystics and magicians had one thing in common—they shared a burning desire for more wisdom, for a hidden knowledge of 'things kept secret from the foundation of the world', for contact with fellow-students of esoteric matters, and when the legend of Christian Rosycross came to them out of Germany they felt that the achievement of this desire was now within their grasp.

'Things are not what they used to be' is a very old saying, for in every age men have felt that they were living on the edge of some vast catastrophe, that the twilight of the Gods was upon them, that previous generations had lived in a world of order and security that had now, alas, gone for ever and had been replaced by an iron age of danger, death, and despair.

Nowhere was the feeling more widespread amongst the literate population nor, perhaps, held with more justification, than in the Germany of the early seventeenth century. The Thirty Years War, that dreadful calamity that was to turn half central Europe into a desert and retard the political development of Germany for two hundred years, was still a few years in the future. Nevertheless, the discerning minority could sense the approaching doom and from the frenzied and competing polemics of Catholic and Calvinist, Lutheran and Anabaptist could dimly guess at the battle, looting and raping that were soon to be upon them. It was within this disturbed and uncertain environment that the members of the Rosicrucian Fraternity (or those who claimed to be such) made the first public announcement of their own existence. This announcement was made in four brief pamphlets published in the years 1614-16.

The first of these pamphlets was the *Fama Fraternitatis*, issued in 1614,[1] along with the second, which was entitled *The General Reformation of the Whole Wide World*. In the following year appeared the *Confessio*; this gave some important dates, but is chiefly remarkable for its extreme Protestant tone and its abuse of what it called 'the asinine brayings of the Pope'. The fourth of the pamphlets was the so-called *Chemical Marriage of Christian Rosycross* which, as will be seen in due course, was either a delightful fairy-tale or, possibly, a beautiful allegory with an inner and mystical meaning.

The *Fama* and the *Confessio* contain brief details of the life of an almost certainly mythical character called Christian Rosy-cross[2] and gave a short history of the Order allegedly founded by him.

The story tells how its hero, son of a German nobleman and product of a monastic education, travelled to Damascus in search of occult knowledge. He did not find what he sought in that city but he did discover that the teachers of a secret wisdom were reputed to dwell 'at Damcar in Arabia'. On his arrival in Damcar he found that his visit was not unexpected for 'the Wise Men received him not as a stranger, but as one whom they had long expected; they called him by his name and showed him other secrets out of his cloister'. During his stay with these Wise Men he improved his Arabic, learnt much physics and mathematics, and translated a mysterious book called 'M' from Arabic into Latin.

Christian Rosycross stayed in Damcar for three years and then, via Egypt, travelled on to Fez, in Morocco, where 'he did get acquainted with those which are commonly called

---

[1] It seems possible that the *Fama* was circulating in manuscript as early as 1610.
[2] The full name is given only in the *Chemical Marriage of Christian Rosycross*, in the other pamphlets he is referred to as Father C.R.C., Brother C.R.C., and simply as C.R.C.

elementary inhabitants[3] who revealed unto him many of their secrets'. He then sailed 'with many costly things into Spain, hoping well, as he himself had so well and profitably spent his time in his travel, that the learned in Europe would highly rejoice with him'—he was disappointed in his hopes, however, and the learned of the University of Salamanca informed him that as the Devil himself had lectured them, they had little to learn from an obscure German wanderer.

The narrative then gives details of the return of Christian Rosycross to Germany and his establishment of the 'Fraternity of the Rosie Cross'—'first by four persons only, and by them was made the magical language and writing, with a large dictionary, which we yet daily use in God's praise and glory'.

The four soon began to make miraculous cures of the sick, and this attracted so many new patients that they decided to double the membership of their Fraternity. This was done and a list of rules was drawn up; these rules were as follows.

1. None of them should profess anything but to cure the sick, and that free of charge.
2. None of the Fraternity should be compelled to wear any particular type of clothing, instead they should adopt the dress of the country in which they were dwelling.
3. The word R.C. should be their seal, mark and character.
4. Every Brother of the Order should choose some worthy person to succeed him on his death.
5. Every year, upon the day of Corpus Christi, they should meet together in the House of the Holy Spirit.
6. The Rosicrucian Fraternity should remain secret for one hundred years.

After this the brethren separated and, it seems, more or less lost sight of one another—the *Fama* says that 'we, who were of the latest, did not know when our loving Father R.C. died'.

The *Fama* then tells the clearly allegorical story of the finding of the Tomb of Christian Rosycross. During the course of

---

[3] This seems to be a reference to the doctrine of elementals—spirits of earth, air, fire and water—which was first fully developed by Paracelsus the sixteenth century alchemist, occultist and physician.

some building operations in the Fraternity's headquarters, the 'House of the Holy Spirit', a large brass nail was revealed which, on being pulled away from the wall, revealed a door on which was written the words POST CCXX ANNOS PATEBO (after 120 years I shall reopen). When the door was eventually opened 'there appeared to our sight a Vault of Seven Sides . . . although the Sun never shined in that Vault, nevertheless it was enlightened with another Sun... and was situated in the upper part in the centre of the ceiling. In the midst . . . was a round altar, covered with a plate of brass, and thereon this engraven "I have made this Tomb a compendium of the Universe". Round the brim were the words "Jesus is all things to me". In the middle were four figures, enclosed in circles, whose circumscription was (1) Nowhere a Vacuum (2) The Burden of the Law (3) The Liberty of the Gospel (4) The Untouched Glory of God. Now as we had not yet seen the body of our careful and wise Father, we therefore removed the altar aside; then we lifted up a strong plate of brass and found a fair and worthy body, whole and unconsumed . . . In his hand he held the book T, the which next unto our Bible is our greatest treasure'. Behind the walls of the Tomb the brethren found books, magical mirrors, bells and even 'ever-burning lamps'.

What was this allegory all about? Well, clearly enough it had at least some connection with a spiritual rebirth, the taking on of new life, an inner resurrection in which 'all things are made new'. Robert Fludd the seventeenth-century Rosicrucian apologist felt this and said:

Some writers have dealt with this mystery (i.e. Resurrection) in dark sayings and methinks the great Rosarius hath described it shrouded in sacred symbols. For here we see a corpse, buried, wherefrom the soul hath gone and seemeth to soar heavenward. The body duly prepared for burial, or even now decaying; yet we see the soul that belongeth thereto, clothed with greater powers, descending to its body. We see a light, as it were the Sun, yet winged and exceeding the Sun of our heaven, arising from the tomb. We see displayed with wondrous courage, a picture of the making of the perfect man.

I shall not waste any time in commenting on the 'General Reformation', for I strongly suspect that it was in no way an authentic Rosicrucian manifesto but was simply bound up with the *Fama* by its enterprising printer. It was, in any case, largely plagiarised from the 'Raguaglio di Parnasso' of Boccalini, an Italian Lutheran who died for his faith in 1613.

The strangest of all these pamphlets was the *Chemical Marriage*, published in 1616—if J. V. Andreae, the Lutheran theologian, was telling the truth when he claimed to have written it at the age of fourteen he was a very unusual and precocious child indeed!

It tells the story of how Christian Rosycross was summoned, one Easter eve, to a royal wedding. On the summons was the Cross, bearing both the solar disc and the lunar crescent, and, although he had been expecting the summons for seven years, Rosycross was so moved that he came near to fainting.

On the following day he woke early and prepared for his journey, putting four red roses in his hat. On the day afterwards he sets off on his journey but finds that there are four roads to the Palace of the King—only one is the Royal Road, but whichever he chooses must be followed to the end, for it is death to turn back. At first Rosycross is undecided which route to choose but, by helping a dove tormented by a raven, eventually finds himself at a large gate carved with many strange and mystical devices. When asked his name he replies that he is a brother of the Red Rosy Cross and, in exchange for water, receives from the porter a gold token and passes on to the second gate which is guarded by a lion. Here he goes through a similar procedure but, in this case, it is the gift of salt which procures him his token. He hurries through the third gate and is just in time for the wedding feast, at the conclusion of which the guests are informed that on the next day they will be weighed in the Great Balance.

Most of the guests fail to pass this test and are given a potion of forgetfulness and turned away from the Palace. Rosycross and a few others pass it, however, and they are invested with the Golden Fleece, summoned to a banquet, and shown the wonders of the Palace which include the Great Phoenix—a symbol of Christ. On the following day the successful candidates attend a banquet but, after they have taken off their white garments and donned black ones, a black man appears, slays the King and Queen and places them in coffins.

Rosycross and his companions then go, under the guidance of a Virgin Teacher, to a seven-storied 'Tower of the Gods' where they immediately begin to prepare material for the 'Great Work'—the magnum opus of the alchemists. This they eventually achieve for, with the aid of blood from the Phoenix, they restore the King and Queen to life and splendour and become 'Knights of the Golden and Rosy Cross'.

This story may, as I have said, be simply a fairy-tale but, in view of the importance assumed by the blood of the Phoenix, a mediaeval symbol of the Christian doctrine of atonement and redemption, and the alchemical symbolism employed, I feel that this is unlikely.

In the last analysis it is quite unimportant whether there was a genuine Rosicrucian Fraternity, from whom the four original pamphlets emanated, or whether the whole thing was either the delusion of a lunatic or the over-elaborate jape of some dedicated practical joker. The important thing is that a great many people believed in the existence of the fraternity, believed that there was a secret body of initiates with supernormal powers, and believed that some day they too might be enabled to enter the ranks of these initiates.

Pamphlets and open letters to the fraternity poured from the presses, begging for Rosicrucian membership; to none of them was vouchsafed a reply or, rather, if any of these writers did get a response they failed to make the fact public, and within a few years the whole subject of Rosicrucianism was regarded with scepticism. Fludd, in England, endeavoured to dispel the rising tide of unbelief.

We of the secret knowledge do wrap ourselves in mystery, to avoid the objurgation and importunity of those who conceive that we cannot be philosophers unless we put our knowledge to some worldly use. There is scarcely one who thinks about us does not believe that our society has no existence; because, as he truly declares, he never met any of us, and he concludes that there is no such brotherhood, because, in his vanity, we seek not him to be our fellow. We do not come, as he assuredly expects, to that conspicuous stage upon which, like himself, as he desires the gaze of the vulgar, every fool may enter: winning order, if the man's appetite be that empty way; and, when he has obtained it, crying out, 'Lo, this is also vanity!'

His efforts were, of course, ineffectual, and by the end of the century both Rosicrucianism and magic were held in some disrepute and it was not until the middle of the eighteenth century that the subjects became once again widely discussed and allegedly Rosicrucian organisations began to appear.

CHAPTER TWO

The Survival and Romanticisation of the Underground Magical Tradition

It was largely through the activities of the astrologers and the so-called 'cunning-men' that popular magic survived in the period 1680-1800. Many of the former dabbled in talismanic magic—the preparation and consecration of amulets designed to undo the effects of unfavourable planetary influences, find lost goods, gain the affection of another, etc.—and in the almanacs issued annually by the better-known astrologers there frequently occur virulent attacks on rivals accused of indulging in such practices.

Not a great deal is known of the cunning-men, the diviners, popular healers, and white witches of the period, for they were discreet in their activities and, as their clients came largely from the peasant and artisan classes, little is to be learnt about them from the periodical literature of the time. They seem to have survived well into the nineteenth century in the more remote parts of England and Wales. John Harries, for example, was born in Carmarthenshire in 1785, and, after unsuccessfully studying medicine in London, he set up in practice as a cunning-man (the Welsh term is dyn hysbys), with clients coming from as far afield as Cardiff. He claimed to derive his secret knowledge largely from his intercourse with

19

the world of spirits, but he also practiced astrology, in which he was a convinced believer, and used a 'magic mirror' for the purpose of obtaining visions. Locally, it was reputed that once a year he retired to a remote spot, drew a magic circle, recited the appropriate conjurations, and had his super-normal powers renewed for a further year by the Devil himself!

His belief in the accuracy of astrological prediction was quite possibly responsible for the piece of accident-proneness that led to his own death. From the study of the planetary positions on the day of his birth he came to the conclusion that there was a 'killing direction' in his horoscope for a certain day in 1839. He consequently retired to his bed, either in the hope of avoiding the coming trouble or, more probably, in order to meet a peaceful end. He was woken up by a cry that the house was on fire, and got up to take part in the fire-fighting, busying himself with carrying buckets of water up to the roof. He slipped and fell from the ladder he was using, thus breaking his neck. He lies buried in Caio church-yard, where his tombstone discreetly describes him as 'John Harries Surgeon'.[1]

It is difficult to know to what extent magic survived in the eighteenth century on a more intellectual and philosophical level. Certainly, however, at least one magician was using the complex Enochian magical system of Dee, for his notebooks have survived, and it is extremely probable that there were others, for when the *Conjuror's Magazine* commenced publication in 1791 it attracted a good deal of correspondence from people whom, while their main interests were astrological, clearly had at least some knowledge of such subjects as ritual magic and alchemy. William Gilbert, a frequent contributor to the magazine, actually tried to make a living by manufacturing talismans. He wrote: 'The manufacture of talismans is a great art, which I have completely mastered after many struggles and oppositions ... I will therefore be PAID, and paid HANDSOMELY.'

[1] He was succeeded in the practice by his son, who himself died some ten years later. Interesting details about both father and son are to be found in Arthur Mee's pamphlet *The Harrieses of Cwrt-y-Cadno*.

He also established, or tried to establish, a school at which would be taught 'Astrology and Spirit with the nature and use of Talismans' at fees varying from £20 to £150 a year. He even seems to have attempted to corner the entire market in talismans (it could not have been a large one) by threatening to discharge and make useless the products of competitors! He advertised that:

No Talismans will for the future be made for any but Pupils, and I will stop the operation of all but those which are made through my own direction or by myself.[2]

A minor revival of dilletante and aristocratic interest in both magic and the other 'hermetic sciences', took place in the late eighteenth century, and this was largely associated with the burgeoning mock-mediaevalism of the Gothic revival. In spite of the fact that it contained instructions for the performance of such pseudo-scientific experiments as producing 'the ghost of a flower' in a vacuum, Ebenezer Sibley's *Celestial Sciences*, which began to be published in 1784, and contained a lengthy section on magic and raising the dead by necromancy, was clearly a product of the same social forces that had been responsible for both the sham-Gothic architecture of Walpole's Strawberry Hill and the literary and financial success of the *Castle of Otranto*.

A far more serious work was Francis Barrett's *The Magus* (1801) which was used as the text book of the school of ritual magic and alchemy which the author established in Marylebone; even in this book, however, the influence of neo-mediaeval romanticism is clearly to be discerned, particularly in the illustrations.

Similar social factors were at work in France. The tarot, that strange pack of seventy-eight playing cards, previously disregarded as being only the tool of gamblers and swindling gipsy fortune-tellers, began to attract the interest of those inclined to antiquarianism. In 1784 Court de Gebelin went

---

[2] Some further information about Gilbert and the magazine for which he wrote can be found in Ellic Howe's fascinating history of modern astrology *Urania's Children*.

so far as to publish a book in which he claimed not only that the tarot symbols were derived from ancient Egypt, but that the whole pack was nothing less than a degenerated version of the Book of Thoth, that legendary repository of all the priestly lore of sacred Khem. His views soon found converts, and by the time of the Revolution, practitioners of cartomancy and other divinatory arts were easily to be found in Paris.

It was not, however, until the mid-nineteenth century that 'Eliphas Zahed Levi' (his real name was Alphonse Louis Constant) made the claim that in some way the tarot cards in general, and the twenty-two trumps of the major arcana in particular, were associated with the Tree of Life, the traditional symbol-system of the Qabalah in both its Hebrew and Christian versions. The major importance of Levi, however, lies not in his cartomantic reveries but in the fact that he was responsible for the surfacing, in an admittedly romanticised form, of the whole underground magical tradition.

Eliphas Levi—for I will use the name by which he preferred to be known—was born in Paris in 1810, the son of a poor shoe-maker. His early childhood was spent in the utmost poverty but, fortunately for himself, he was an extremely intelligent child—one who knew him as a boy described him as 'eating books'—and he escaped from his miserable environment via the traditional route of the seminary of Saint Sulpice and a free training for the Catholic Priesthood.

Even as a young seminarian Eliphas Levi was rebellious; Marie Gebhard, a pupil of his who later became a Theosophist, has left a description of his anti-authoritarian acts and the punishments to which he was consequently subjected by his ecclesiastical Superiors. Nevertheless, he easily passed the customary examinations—in any case they were not particularly onerous at that period—and became a Deacon. He failed to go on to the Priesthood, however, for he developed what were described as 'strange doctrines'; none of those who have written of Levi seem to know what these doctrines were, but I am now reasonably satisfied that Levi had become a convert to the peculiar half-religious, half-political doctrines of that lunatic fringe of extremist 'French royalism' which later became known as the 'Saviours of Louis XVII'.

In about 1838 Levi became friendly with Alphonse Esquiros a bizarre romantic, who later published a novel, *The Magician*, the characters of which included a whole harem of female zombies, a brass robot which preached incessantly of the virtues of chastity and an hermaphrodite which carried on a correspondence with the moon! It was through Esquiros that, in 1839, Levi met Ganneau, whose disciple he became.

Ganneau preached a sort of revolutionary royalism—he believed that in some sense he was a reincarnation of Louis XVII and his wife of Marie Antoinette—and Levi became a wandering missionary for his sect, suffering what he called 'great persecution' in 1843 and actual imprisonment in 1847. Eventually Levi became disillusioned with this pseudo-Messiah, although not before writing the *Gospel of Liberty*, a religious-cum-Socialist tract whose ravings about tyrants' skulls filled with blood etc. are reminiscent of Lamennais at his very worst. After this he made a living by journalistic hack-work—he wrote a whole volume for the large and ultra-montane *Dictionary of the Christian Religion*.

Early in the 'fifties Levi wrote his *Dogma and Ritual of High Magic*—although the *Dogma* and the *Ritual* were published separately, in 1854 and 1856 respectively, internal evidence makes it fairly certain that they were originally written as one book.

In *Dogma and Ritual* and the major works that followed it— *History of Magic* and *Key of the Great Mysteries*—Levi completely romanticised the whole magical and alchemical tradition, the interpretation of the tarot cards, and what little he knew of the Hebrew Qabalah. The descriptive phrase that springs to mind on reading Levi's books is 'nineteenth century Gothic', they are a literary-occult version of St. Pancras Station and, it may be added, like the architecture of St. Pancras, their style is once again becoming fashionable.[3] I will give only one example of Levi's Gothicisation of the magical tradition; the

---

[3] The literary pedigree of the hippy-occult magazine *Gandalf's Garden* could aptly be described as being by Levi out of Henry Miller—but I suspect that its contributors are unaware of their line of descent.

late mediaeval *Grimoire of Honorius*, falsely attributed to the Pope of that name, gives a formula for evoking the 'Kings of the Four Quarters and the Angels of the Days of the Week'. In all the versions I have seen of this grimoire the operation is preceded by the lighting of a large fire in an isolated place and tracing a magical circle with the aid of a crucifix. In his *History of Magic* he describes this simple activity in the following terms:

In a sinister place, by the light of a fire kindled with broken crucifixes, a circle is traced with the embers of a burnt crucifix, reciting while doing so a magical hymn containing verses from the psalms of David.

Levi was no mere Gothic vulgariser, however, and in his books he made high claims for the antiquity and validity of the magical tradition. Thus he stated that magic was of undoubted potency and that its traditions held, under concealing veils, the real secrets of good and evil; that the traditional doctrines of magic were alone capable of adequately explaining the phenomena of spiritualism and the deeper aspects of hyponotism; and that beneath the shadowing symbolism of all exoteric and popular religion lay the doctrines of magic, the only universally valid religion.

At first Levi's books seem to have made little impact, but, as the years passed, they attracted readers who desired to practice the magical doctrines that Levi preached, and some of these would-be magicians were English.

CHAPTER THREE

Masonic Rosicrucians

While the earlier interest in the Rosicrucian Fraternity and the higher aspects of magic had been largely confined to professional scholars, in the eighteenth century such interests were to be found amongst the members of both aristocratic and bourgeois Masonic Lodges, and were a notable preoccupation of those freemasons affiliated to the continental high-grades.

It seems that within a very few years of the publication of the *Fama* some people had drawn the conclusion that there was a connection between Rosicrucianism and Freemasonry, for as early as 1638 the following lines occur in Adamson's *Muses Threnody*.

> For what we do presage is not in grosse,
> For we be brethren of the Rosie Crosse;
> We have the Mason Word and second sight
> Things for to come we can foretell aright.

I think it of some significance that this quotation comes from a Scot who was himself probably a Freemason. For Scotland was the home of speculative—that is to say occult and philosophical—masonry, as distinct from the crude operative masonry that was a forerunner of modern trade-unionism, and I am inclined to believe that as early as the seventeenth century some form of Rosicrucian degree was being worked by certain Scottish Masonic Lodges,[1] this degree being the ancestor of both the 'Rose-Croix 18°' of the 'Ancient and Accepted Rite'

[1] My belief is a most unorthodox one and would not be shared by the majority of reputable masonic historians.

and the R.S.Y.C.S. (Rosy Cross) degree of the modern masonic 'Royal Order of Scotland'.

Be that as it may, it is certain that by the fifth decade of the eighteenth century Scottish Jacobite exiles were working an allegedly Rosicrucian masonic rite and that this rite was the direct ancestor of the contemporary masonic degree known as the *Rose-Croix of Heredom*.

Certain masonic historians, anxious to free their 'craft' from any taint of occultism, have stated that there is no connection between this degree on the one hand and the Rosicrucian Fraternity and its philosophy on the other. They have unquestionably given their verdict against the evidence; for once I find myself in agreement with A. E. Waite who wrote:

I am personally convinced that the whole arrangement of the Rose-Croix Grade; its clothing, its jewel, its entire mise-en-scene, the chambers in which it is worked are reminiscent of the older Order. The three points are in crude correspondence with the Hermetic work in Alchemy—blackness, death, and finally resurrection into the red or perfect state. . . . It follows that the various Masonic writers who have denied any connection between the Eighteenth Degree and the Rosicrucian Order have either spoken with an extraordinary absence of even elementary knowledge or with considerable want of sincerity. The bond of kinship lies upon the surface of the subject, and those who have eyes can scarcely fail to see.

Added to this it must be said that there are strong resemblances between certain aspects of this degree and the story told in the *Chemical Marriage of Christian Rosycross*. For example, the apron worn by the mason has embroidered upon it a Pelican feeding its young with blood.[2] Now the Pelican and the Phoenix were interchangeable symbols in mediaeval times, and, it will be remembered, it was with blood of a Phoenix that Christian Rosycross restored the King and Queen to life.

While it would be hotly denied by the Bishops and other

[2] A Pelican also appears on the collar and the jewel of this degree.

26

Church of England clergymen who are members of the 18°, there is no doubt at all in my mind that, even in its watered-down twentieth-century version the *Rose Croix of Heredom*[3] teaches a doctrine of initiation and spiritual rebirth that must immediately derive from the Rosicrucians and ultimately from the later Gnostics and Neo-Platonists. I am inclined to agree with an anti-masonic writer who said:

> ... a Docetic Christology underlies this degree. ... Christ's death and resurrection appear to be regarded, not as an objective act of redemption, but rather as a type of the experiences which the initiate must undergo in his quest for illumination. The emphasis seems to be on the initiate's ... achieving his own salvation through enlightenment.... The initiate gives his age as thirty-three, whatever it may be in reality. He travels for thirty-three days in seven concentric circles representing the seven periods of the world's existence. He passes through the blackness of death to his resurrection in the Red Room, and ascends the ladder to glory and perfection. He hears the Resurrection in the Closing ceremony described as the hour of a perfect Mason. This seems a little sinister, but far less so than the description of Our Lord's triumphant redemptive death on the Cross as a dire calamity for Masonry—a phrase which carried the unfortunate suggestion that the death of Satan is being mourned.[4]

This Rose-Croix degree was worked in England as early as the late eighteenth century, but as a masonic Order in its own right, not as a mere part of some larger system. This independent Rose-Croix was probably under the patronage of Sir Thomas Dunckerley, an illegitimate son of George II, who was also chief of the quasi-masonic Templar encampments.

---

[3] The real meaning of the word Heredom has obsessed several masonic historians. The most popular explanation is that it is derived from the Greek words hieros domos (holy house) but it almost certainly has its origin in an eighteenth century French legend that there was a Mount Heredom in Scotland in which the secrets of the Rosy Cross were preserved.

[4] I feel it advisable to state that, while I think this writer's description of the 18° admirably sums up its neo-Gnostic, Rosicrucian doctrine of initiation, I do not share the High Anglican viewpoint from which it is written.

In 1865 another masonic-Rosicrucian body, the Societas Rosicruciana in Anglia (Rosicrucian Society in England), was formed by Robert Wentworth Little upon the basis of old manuscripts allegedly found in Freemasons' Hall. The rituals derived from those manuscripts bore a faint relationship to those of the German 'Fratres of the Golden and Rosy Cross', a late eighteenth-century Rosicrucian organisation whose membership, like that of its later English imitator, was confined to Master Masons.

An early member of the 'Soc. Ros.', as the society was usually known, was Kenneth R. H. Mackenzie, a young mason and occultist who claimed that he had been initiated into a continental Rosicrucian fraternity by an Austrian named Count Apponyi—it is interesting to note that someone of this name was attached to the Austrian Embassy in Paris at a time when it is known that Mackenzie was also there. Mackenzie was a pupil of Fred Hockley, a great collector of ancient magical texts, who had himself been the pupil of a member of Francis Barrett's magical school, and it was Hockley who ensured that a short time after his protegé visited Eliphas Levi in Paris, he noted down his memories of the conversations that had taken place. Ten years later Mackenzie wrote an important article for the *Rosicrucian*, the short-lived magazine of the Soc. Ros., and in this he gave not only some interesting, personal reminiscences of Levi but also an exposition of his personal attitude towards the magical arts: [5]

> Magic is not a necromanteia—a raising of dead material substances endowed with an imagined life—but a psychological branch of science, dealing with the sympathetic effects of stones, drugs, herbs, and living substances upon the imaginative and reflective faculties—and leading to ever new glimpses of the world of wonders around us, ranking

[5] This quotation is lengthy, perhaps excessively so; nevertheless I feel it best to give it here, rather than to confine it to an appendix, as it illustrates so well (a) the way in which Mackenzie and those of similar views managed to reconcile a belief in traditional magic with an acceptance of nineteenth century science; (b) the veneration in which Eliphas Levi was held, and (c) the connecting temporal links between the French romanticisation of occultism and the later English magicians.

28

it in due order of phenomena, and illustrating the benefi-
cence of The Great Architect of the Universe. Magic, therefore, is a legitimately masonic field of study, and in these
days, where practical chemistry produces alcohol from flint
stones, surely we may not be very astonished at the possibility of obtaining spiritual truth from the interrelations of
material substances. In such wise acted the elder alchemists,
to whom the proud modern chemist, wrapt in ineffable
disdain of their labours, but whence he sprang, will give no
praise and no ear. Politically speaking, the old methods might
be considered as the conservative aspect of science—the
modern utilitarian—the liberal—and both, in a sense, are
true—proceeding in different ratios of speed in parallel lines,
or so infinitely remote in consequence as to be inappreciable
to human thought.

Let us then honour such men who seek, with devotion
and humility, to harmonize the two sides of the great veil
of Isis, which no man has, in mortal life, ever been able to
lift. Dimly, under the fringe, scintillations of the life beyond
may be seen, and the rapt vision of the seer—the Roch—
may perhaps be gifted enough to behold the outlines of the
glory which burns for ever in the presence of the Ancient
of Days.

Having left London, therefore, on the 25th of November,
1861, I occupied myself, on arriving in Paris, with an investigation as to the state of occult studies in that city. Among
others, of whom, at some future time, I may give an account
to the Society, I desired much to visit Eliphas Levi Zahed—
known to men as the Abbé Alphonse Louis Constant, the
author of several works connected with the Holy Cabbala,
and with Occult Philosophy and Illuminism.

On the morning of the 3rd of December, 1861, I therefore
repaired to the residence of Eliphas Levi, situated at No. 19,
Avenue de Maine. The building proved to be a handsome
and well arranged structure of brick, with a square garden
in front, handsome gate, porter's lodge, and generally good
approaches—the building being three stories high. Upon
enquiring of the porter, I found that Eliphas Levi resided

29

upon the second floor, the first floor, probably, being offices of some kind. There I found a narrow passage in which there were four doors to my right, apparently opening upon a number of small rooms. On the fourth door I perceived a small card about three inches long, upon which were inscribed some Hebrew characters equivalent to Eliphas Levi (Alphonse Louis); in each corner was one of the four letters forming the sacred word INRI, and the whole of this Hebrew inscription was written in the three primitive colours— viz: red, yellow, and blue.

It was about ten a.m. when I knocked, and the door was opened by Eliphas Levi himself. I found him a short burly man, with a rubicund complexion, very small but piercing eyes twinkling with good humour, his face broad, his lips small and well compressed together, nostrils dilating. The lower part of his face was covered with a thick black beard and moustache, and I noticed that his ears were small and delicate. In person he was lusty, and his dress was plain and quiet. Upon his head he wore a kind of felt hat turned up in front. On his removing his hat to salute me, I observed that his head was partially bald, his hair dark and glistening, and that portion of his skull, which had been submitted to the tonsure, was partially overgrown with hair.

He apologized for wearing his hat, stating that he was compelled to do so by an affection of his head, which rendered it dangerous for him to remain uncovered.

Having briefly stated my name and presented my credentials, I proceeded to express my gratification at the information I had derived from the perusal of his works, and I told him that my mission to him was to learn the state of his studies, insofar as he might feel disposed to inform me, and at the same time to give him the latest intelligence of the condition of occult studies in England. He replied, in French, that language, Latin and Hebrew, being the only languages known to him, that he was highly pleased to receive any stranger whose studies were akin to his own, and that he had the satisfaction of knowing that his works upon Philosophical Magic had obtained for him the sympathy of many inquiring minds in all parts of Europe.

Among his disciples, Eliphas Levi especially mentioned, the Count Braszynsky, the Polish millionaire, to whom, he said, he was indebted for a variety of the manuscripts then in his possession. I said that I had been, for some time, making collections in reference to the occult game of Tarot, and that I wished particularly to learn whether he proposed to carry out the intention expressed in the 'Rituel et Dogme de la Haute Magie' of issuing a complete set of Tarot cards.

He replied that he was very willing to do so—and took from among his manuscripts a small volume in which were depicted the twenty-one cards of the Tarot with the Zero or Fool, according to the earliest authorities. Those cards were drawn by his own hand, and the little volume contained a large number of the symbols of Theurgia and Goetia, a medley of collections from the Key of Rabbi Solomon and similar occult repertories.

This little work (he told me) had cost him twenty years to put together. He was kind enough to state that if I had any intention of publishing, in England, any set of Tarot cards, I might count upon him for all assistance, and that he would supply me with all drawings and instructions for their use.

After this preliminary conversation our discourse became general, and then, for the first time, I ventured to take a glance at his apartment.

The room is small and irregular in shape, and its dimensions appear all the less from the fact of its being crowded with furniture. In a recess behind his usual writing table, was a species of altar, with a set of gilt vessels such as are usually used in Roman Catholic Churches in the celebration of the Mass. Sumptuous drapery of yellow and drab covered this piece of furniture, in the centre of which lay a Hebrew roll of the Law; above it was a gilt triangle bearing the name of Jehovah; on the right side of this altar was a species of sideboard, also hung with drapery. Under a glass case I noticed a manuscript of talismans, as I perceived from the pages that were open.

Next to this came the window, having a northern aspect, and close to it was placed the ordinary writing table of Eliphas Levi—a large and substantial piece of furniture, with shelves in front, covered with books and manuscripts. Behind, on the wall, next to the writing table and close to the window, hung a life-size picture representing a female, her hands clasped to her bosom, adoring the Sacred Word, which appeared in a kind of glory.

Eliphas then informed me that the female represented the Holy Cabbala. Underneath the picture was an antique sofa, with red velvet cushions. At the end of the room was the fire-place, before which a curiously contrived screen was placed. The mantle-shelf was loaded with a series of massive looking vases, in which were coins, medallions, and talismans. On the other side of the fire-place, opposite the picture was a smaller cabinet with glass doors, hung with red drapery, with shelves above, on which were ranged books not of an occult character. Within the cabinet I saw a number of manuscripts, printed books, talismans, a glass water vessel of a blue colour, two skulls, and a variety of other magical apparatus.

Next to this cabinet came the door, upon which was suspended a large cabbalistical diagram, of which Eliphas Levi informed me that only one hundred impressions had been taken. Upon the walls were suspended many engravings and paintings having reference to the Cabbala. The whole room was profusely decorated with hangings of every kind, and presented an effective theatrical appearance. Upon one of the side boards I noticed an Egyptian figure of Isis, upon which I commented as being very perfect, at which Eliphas Levi laughed, and told me it was an article of commerce in Paris, being, in fact, a very large tobacco jar.

We conversed upon the subject of Theosophy considerably, and Eliphas Levi did me the favour to remark that the form of my head was evidently that of a person greatly given to such studies. Eliphas Levi informed me that if there were any truths to be discovered in his books—as he believed there were—they were not to be attributed to his own wisdom, but that he had arrived at the various inductions there published by means of the combinations presented by the twenty-two cards of the Tarot. He also mentioned that those works had been prepared for the press by a friend, he himself not possessing the requisite literary ability.

Altogether my impression upon my first visit was highly favourable; his manner was simple, sincere and straightforward. He spoke to me of his visit to England, stating his inability to speak English, a language he had in vain endeavoured to acquire—he rendered a tribute to the versatile knowledge of Lord, then Sir Edward Bulwer, Lytton, with emphasis. I asked him, among other questions, whether he recognised the existence, as a fact, of a means of communication with departed spirits. His reply was this:

'Break a bottle of oil under water, at however remote a distance from the surface, the mass of oil will ascend to that surface, while the remains of the bottle will sink to the bottom. Thus,' he continued, 'do I conceive that the soul, upon quitting the body, by its spiritual specific gravity, ascends to the sphere for which it is destined. Like the oil, it remains ever uppermost, and returns not to earth.'

I then urged upon him that spirits might, by refraction, or reflection, communicate with earth, but I found him an utter materialist upon this question. Time was now drawing on, I therefore bade him adieu, fixing the next morning for a resumption of our converse.

On my second interview, the following morning, he reiterated all his friendly expressions, and proceeded with great kindness to show me a variety of manuscripts of his own and of other persons. One work he laid before me was a photographic copy of a printed book, the title-page of which was unknown to him, having been torn off; it was, however, a prophecy by the celebrated Paracelsus, illustrated with symbolical figures, and predicting, in unmistakable language, the first French revolution, the rise of Napoleon, the downfall of the Papacy, the restoration of the kingdom of Italy, the abrogation of the temporal power of the Pope, the downfall of the clergy, and the ultimate ascendancy of the occult sciences, as a means of restoring general harmony in society.

The work is an octavo, containing thirty-two chapters, and the copy I saw was one of six taken by the Count Braszynsky from the imperfect original, which the possessor, a gentleman residing in Warsaw, would not sell to the Count, although he offered him any money he wished to ask for it. Some portion of the work has been quoted by Eliphas Levi, in *La Clef des Grandes Mystères*, p. 378 and 99.

The mention of the name of Paracelsus led me to remark upon the talismanic nature of many of his medical preparations, and I commented upon the effect these talismans produced either upon the imagination or otherwise. Eliphas Levi then proceeded to relate to me the following singular vision:

'Among the various works of Paracelsus which have been published, is one consisting almost entirely of talismans and sigils; I had been much surprised at finding no reference in that work directly or indirectly to the subject of the Tarot, a subject which has engaged my whole life, and which, originally contained in the book Zohar, has come down to our time in the form in which I showed it you yesterday.'

I here interposed, and said:—'Excuse me, but I have a great curiosity about the work Zohar. Can you tell me whether it has been printed, and if so, at what time?'

Eliphas Levi replied:—'To give you any idea of the volume of the book Zohar, I should tell you that a very large cart would not contain it. It is, in fact, an extended commentary upon the entire works of the Old Testament, and was written long prior to the foundation of the Masoretic system of writing with points, and even before the invention of the Samaritan character. It was written in a character which has remained to our day, and has formed the substratum from which the various uncouth characters of sigils have resulted.'

At this Eliphas Levi took out his manuscript work upon the Tarot, and there showed me the original characters. I then asked him kindly to resume.

'I had retired to rest, and with the lamp beside me was

engaged in turning over the leaves of the work of Paracelsus (named Archidoxis). Overcome by sleep, I fell into an unconscious state, and in that condition found myself in a large hall, filled with alchymical apparatus, with draperies and signs appertaining to the laboratory of an occult philosopher.

'I was gazing upon the scene, to me more complete than anything I had ever witnessed, when I found myself confronted by a majestic form; a man stood before me, whose stature was evidently greater than my own, attired in a long robe, with a girdle round his waist, and a fillet on his hair about the temples. His face wore an expression of mockery, mingled with good nature, and he addressed me, welcoming me to his hall of audience. I conversed with him for some time, and told him that "over yonder" I had been engaged in studying his works, for I felt a conviction that it was Paracelsus in whose presence I stood. I remarked upon the fact that I found no reference to the Tarot in his works; but I observed that I could not imagine him ignorant of that important subject. At the waist of Paracelsus there hung a small pouch, and from it, in reply, he drew a copper coin. The coin I have described in one of my works. It represents the first figure of the Tarot, the Bateleur or juggler—before him is a table on which are displayed the various symbols of his art.

'I remarked to Paracelsus that I longed to possess such a rare and beautiful coin; upon which he replied that it was impossible to present me with that particular example of it. I asked him whether "over yonder" it was possible to obtain one, to which he answered by bidding me follow him. I did so, and passing through a smaller hall, we emerged into the street. I then, for the first time, perceived that we were in Paris, and I noted with astonishment, that the strange attire of my companion attracted no attention from the numerous passers by; I therefore concluded that to them we were invisible. Passing from street to street, we at length came to the Pont Neuf, and he then told me he would be able to give me such a coin, as I should possess "over yonder".

35

He stooped down in the broad daylight, and began to scrape away the earth between two stones. After thus removing the surface, he took from the fissure a coin or metal exactly similar to the one he had produced from his pouch, and he handed this to me, bidding me place in the fissure one sou, which I did. He then covered up the place, and in my joy at having received the medal I awoke.

'I confess that upon my waking I positively felt in my waistcoat pocket, in which I had placed the coin in my dream, to see if it were there. I need not say I was disappointed. The matter, however, preyed upon my mind. I rose early the next day, and I confess to you with shame that my weakmindness was such, that I went at once to the Pont Neuf, to see whether I should find the coin by digging in the earth.

'When I arrived there, the whole vision, with the passengers around me, seemed familiar—in fact, to realize my dream. I positively recognized the two stones between which my invisible guide had discovered the coin. I eagerly stooped down, and scraped away the earth. I need not tell you that I found no coin there; but, on resuming my erect position, my eye glanced upon the stall of a curiosity dealer hard by. I was irresistibly led to the stall, and found a number of coins, and among them,' said Eliphas Levi, holding up the medal in triumph to me, 'I discovered the exact fac-simile of the coin produced by Paracelsus in the vision.'

'You may be able,' I then said to Eliphas Levi, 'to supply me with some means of judging the causes of this vision.'

His remark, in reply, was this:—'I have no doubt that upon purely natural causes the whole of this singular vision may be explained. I had fallen asleep with the work of Paracelsus in my hand—what more natural than that my mind should recur to such circumstances as I knew connected with him?'

I said:—'But how do you explain the matter of the coin? Did you know of the existence of such a thing?'

Eliphas Levi replied:—'I did not.'

'Then,' I said, 'how was it that by such a happy intuition,

in a vision you perceived that which you were afterwards to purchase in reality? You say you are no spiritualist, yet it seems to me, this ought almost to convert you.'

He replied:—'I was well acquainted with the fact that the coin dealer habitually exposed his wares on the quay beside the bridge. I had often passed the stall, yet I confess I had never to my knowledge seen the coin. The matter is inexplicable to me. I relate the circumstances to you faithfully as they occurred—and here is the coin.'

I then narrated to Eliphas Levi, in return for his vision, a few instances of realised dreams. Among other topics of conversation, I especially inquired whether he had any works he proposed to publish at a future time. He replied, by producing a handsomely bound quarto volume, written by his own hand, in blue ink, irregularly and stragglingly. Each page was illustrated by drawings, chiefly presenting an intermixture of the primary colours, red, yellow, and blue. Through these were fancifully drawn the ordinary cabbalistic figures engraved in his works. This volume contained commentaries on the books of Ezekiel and the Apocalypse, which he connected directly with the prophecy of Paracelsus he had already shown me.

From one of his numerous receptacles he produced a remarkable Cabbalistic plate, which he had bought upon one of the quays. Respecting this plate, he informed me that in a manuscript record, in the possession of his friend, the Count Braszynsky, and attributed to the renowned Cagliostro, a prediction had been made that a certain person would arise in the nineteenth century, who should be able clearly to express the meaning of this plate, and in the manuscript the name of the person was given as Alphonse; this Eliphas Levi attributed to himself.

Eliphas Levi and myself also conversed respecting the Urim and Thummim, and the breast-plate of Aaron. Upon this Eliphas Levi referred to the small hand-book formerly named, and there showed me a drawing of the Ark of the Covenant, with the four symbolic figures at the corners. He then bade me notice that the top of the ark was a plane surface, and that it was large enough to allow the rectangular breast-plate of the High Priest to turn freely round in any direction. He then told me he had discovered the method of using the Urim and Thummim to be as follows:

The breast-plate of the High Priest, it is known, contained twelve stones, each cut into six fascets or sides; upon each was engraven one of the seventy-two names of God. Thus the Urim and Thummim contained the whole Cabbala. Upon its being placed at the top of the ark, the High Priest, offering up a prayer for enlightenment, turned the breast-plate round upon itself, and, upon its ceasing to revolve, the High Priest watched the reflection of the four animals in the stone of the tribe whom the question concerned, and, combining them with the Divine Name, drew his conclusions.

I finally parted with Eliphas Levi, with the greatest assurances of good feeling on his part, and his testimony of satisfaction at being informed of the present condition of magical and other studies in England; he reiterated to me his offers of service, and requested me to correspond with him upon any topics that might seem of interest to both.

On the whole the early members of the Societas Rosicruciana were a second-rate lot, and, with a few exceptions they seem to have had little knowledge of the inner nature and teachings of traditional Rosicrucianism. This is illustrated by their whole-hearted admiration of Hargrave Jennings and his odd book *The Rosicrucians, their Rites and Mysteries*. This extraordinary book is concerned almost exclusively with phallicism and phallic images—Jennings saw the penis everywhere. Round towers in Ireland, dolmens, cromlechs, the designs on Gnostic gems; all these, according to Jennings, were symbols of the male organ and were also, in some strange and undefinable manner, connected with Rosicrucianism. He even believed that England's premier order of chivalry, the Order of the Garter, was originally a phallic cult; he suggested that its motto 'honi soit qui mal y pense' had originally read 'yoni soit qui mal y pense'—which could, I suppose, be loosely translated as 'people who think evil are c——s'!

CHAPTER FOUR

Dr. Westcott and a Goat

In the latter half of the nineteenth century two exotic and seemingly new developments of traditional occultism attracted widespread interest in England. They were American spiritualism, in many ways merely the old cult of necromancy in a nineteenth-century guise, and Madame Blavatsky's Theosophy, a watered down synthesis of Hindu and Buddhist religion. Modern spiritualism originated with a family named Fox and the 'Hydesville knockings' of 1848. The Foxes were a comparatively poor family living in a wooden house at Hydesville, Wayne, New York State. The daughters, Margeretta and Kate, shared a bedroom together, and, centred on this bedroom, came an outbreak of mysterious knocking, rappings and other typical poltergeist activity. According to their own account the Foxes, with remarkable stolidity, soon became fairly used to these disturbances. and it was not until one of the daughters rapped back at the noisy spirit, subsequently agreeing with it on a simple code, that they began to attach any great importance to their peculiar experiences.

By means of the simple alphabetic code that had been agreed upon, the spirit—if, indeed, it was a spirit and not, as has been suggested, the rhythmical crackings of the joints of the sisters' big toes—announced that it was the ghost of a pedlar, murdered by the previous owner in the room now occupied by the girls, and buried in the cellar. Tremendous excitement followed, the house was besieged with curious visitors, including journalists, and rappings and other phenomena no longer confined themselves to the house, but followed the girls elsewhere. The excitement increased still further when some bones were

39

allegedly found in the cellar, but abated somewhat when the bones produced were found to be of animal origin, and the indignant former owner of the house turned up, indignantly denying any knowledge of either the pedlar or his supposed murder.

Soon other people began to get the same phenomena, and to open up 'communication with the spirit-world' by means of raps, the ouija board, and the planchette. Spiritualism became a craze, at first only in America but, ultimately, in England and Western Europe also.

Two American mediums, Mrs. Haydon and Mrs. Roberts, visited England as early as 1852, making many converts, and, in 1855, Daniel Dunglas Home,[1] offspring of an irregular liaison between the eleventh Earl of Home and a Southampton chambermaid, and thus by blood the great-uncle of Sir Alec Douglas-Home, commenced his extraordinary mediumistic career. His levitations, materialisations, and other amazing, if possibly fraudulent, phenomena created a considerable aristocratic and upper middle-class following for himself and other, less eminent, professional mediums.

Spiritualism also spread rapidly among the working class; the conversion of Robert Owen, the old utopian socialist and real originator of the co-operative movement, was probably largely responsible for this, for he still retained a certain personal following among the more literate sections of the artisan community, particularly in the north of England. By 1855 the *Yorkshire Spiritual Telegraph*, England's first spiritualist journal, was established and, while it did not enjoy a long life, it is fairly clear that it was intended to reach a working- and lower middle-class readership.

Thirty years after the introduction of spiritualism into England, A. P. Sinnett's book *The Occult World* became widely read, and it led some into an acceptance of the oriental occultism of Madame Blavatsky's Theosophical Society, the London Lodge of this organisation being founded in January 1883. The Theosophical Society had a much narrower appeal than the earlier importation, and its social base was solidly middle-class. There

[1] He was, of course, the original of Browning's 'Mr. Sludge, the Medium'.

was a certain overlap with spiritualism, however, and the well-known medium Mabel Collins joined the new movement. In 1888 a group of professional fortune-tellers in Yorkshire began to publish an occult magazine called the *Lamp of Thoth*. Some, at least, of these fortune-tellers appear to have been followers of Hiram Butler, the American advocate of free love, food reform and spiritualism; for one who called himself 'a victim' wrote: 'The Society is composed chiefly of Spiritualists and bogus Astrologers, who delight in taking money from servant girls, and there are men in the Society who are blind followers of Hiram Butler of America.' It was a markedly inferior production, and, although I have only been able to trace one surviving copy of the magazine, I am inclined to agree with 'one who has been duped' who described its contents as 'all pilfered from Books of Black Magic'. Nevertheless, it attracted notice at the time because some of the articles were signed 'Secretary Ros. Crux', thus appearing to have a Rosicrucian origin. Subsequently it became known that this same secretary had acquired a goat, which he proposed to sacrifice at the next full meeting of his society. Soon afterwards a furious letter appeared in the Theosophical magazine *Lucifer* denouncing the Yorkshire occultists and declaring that they were in no way whatsoever connected with Rosicrucianism. This denunciation was signed by W. Wynn Westcott, who, no doubt to the puzzlement of most of the readers of *Lucifer*, described himself as the 'Praemonstrator of the Hermetic Order of the G.D.'.

The indignant Yorkshiremen replied that (a) a goat was no longer kept, (b) Ros. Crux meant only 'Dew and Light' and (c) that Freemasons ate a great deal too much. Shortly afterwards both the Yorkshiremen and their magazine vanished into that obscurity in which they have ever since remained, but it is this curious controversy which led to the first discreet announcement of the connection of Westcott with the Hermetic Order of the Golden Dawn, an organisation whose activities and teachings were largely responsible for the survival of ritual magic in both Great Britain and the U.S.A. and whose members included W. B. Yeats, poet and Nobel prize winner, Florence Farr, actress and one-time mistress of George Bernard Shaw, and Aleister Crowley, poet, mountaineer, and daemonic prophet of the new religion of Thelema.

There is a certain mystery attached to the origins of the Order; at least three versions of the events that led to its foundation are known to me—I have a strong reason to believe that the one I give is correct but, needless to say, I may be wrong.

Three of the four founder-members of the Golden Dawn were also members of the Societas Rosicruciana in Anglia. The fourth, the Rev. A. F. A. Woodford, had been a close friend of Kenneth R. H. MacKenzie and was, in fact, the compiler of much of the latter's *Masonic Cyclopaedia*. Woodford had taken his Licentiateship in Theology at Durham and, after some years as a country vicar, had taken up residence in Notting Hill where he also held a curacy. When Fred Hockley the mystic, clairvoyant and would-be magician died in 1885 some of his papers passed into the hands of Woodford who found among them certain manuscripts in cypher. This discovery does not seem to have unduly excited him, for while he mentioned their existence to Westcott in February 1886, it was not until the summer of the following year that he sent them to Westcott for his considered opinion.

By September 1887 Westcott had managed to decode the manuscripts. It could not have been a particularly difficult task, although, perhaps, a laborious one; for the cipher appears in an easily-available seventeenth-century English work and was, I believe, derived originally from the 'Polygraphia' of the great Abbot Trithemius. They proved to be a skeletonic description,[2] in English, of five hitherto unknown rituals of a Rosicrucian nature which the writer had witnessed—presumably in Germany, as the manuscript also contained the address of a certain Anna Sprengel of Nuremburg, allegedly a high-grade Rosicrucian.[3]

Westcott was excited by his discovery and called in S. L.

[2] See Appendix A—*The Cipher Manuscripts*.
[3] The dates given in these last two paragraphs I have derived from (a) an alleged copy of Westcott's diary for the period in question and (b) a copy of the official history lecture of the Stella Matutina seemingly annotated by Westcott *circa* 1918.

MacGregor Mathers, already gaining a good reputation for scholarship in occult matters, to give a second opinion. Mathers reported favourably on the manuscripts and Westcott asked for his co-operation in working up the bare bones of the system into a coherent whole suitable for Lodge-work. Mathers agreed to this and was also responsible for bringing in a certain Dr. W. R. Woodman as a third co-worker.

In October of the same year Westcott wrote to Fräulein Sprengel at the address given and, in due course, a reply was received, thus commencing a voluminous correspondence. Much occult teaching was given, honorary grades of Exempt Adept ($7° = 4°$) were conferred upon Westcott, Mathers and Woodman, and a Charter was given for the establishment of a Golden Dawn Temple to work the five grades outlined in the cypher manuscripts. Thus, in 1888, the Isis-Urania Temple of the Golden Dawn came into existence. Its foundation came at a time when many people were beginning to be dissatisfied with the pathetically over-confident materialism of the nineteenth-century science on one hand, and the fatuous pietism of fundamentalist religion on the other. Those who had been attracted by the spiritual and intellectual content of Blavatsky's Theosophy but repelled by its oriental form began to find their way into the Golden Dawn. Within a short time the Isis-Urania Temple in London had been joined by the Osiris Temple in Weston-super-Mare, the Horus Temple in Bradford and the Amen-Ra Temple in Edinburgh. A few years later Mathers founded the Ahathoor Temple in Paris.

In 1891 the correspondence with Anna Sprengel suddenly ceased; a communication from Germany informed Westcott that (a) his correspondent was dead, (b) that her companions had not approved of (though not interfered with) her teaching activities, and (c) that no further information would be given to the English students—if they wished to establish a link with the Secret Chiefs of the Order they must do it themselves.

In 1892 Mathers claimed to have established such a link, and supplied rituals for a Second Order, the Red Rose and the Cross of Gold, based on the traditional story of the finding of

43

the tomb of Christian Rosycross. These rituals were adopted and a 'Vault of the Adepts' became the controlling force behind the Temples of the Golden Dawn in the Outer. Mathers has left his own description of how he made his contact with the Secret Chiefs and constructed his rituals:

Prior to the establishment of the Vault of the Adepts in Britannia it was found absolutely and imperatively necessary that there should be some eminent member especially chosen to act as the link between the Secret Chiefs and the more external forms of the Order. It was requisite that such a member should be me, who, while having the necessary and peculiar educational basis of critical and profound Occult Archaeological knowledge should at the same time be not only ready but willing to devote himself in every sense to a blind and unreasoning obedience to those Secret chiefs....

Concerning the Secret Chiefs of the Order, to whom I make reference and from whom I have received the wisdom of the Second Order, which I have communicated to you, I can tell you *nothing*. I know not even their earthly names. I know them only by certain secret mottos I have but very rarely seen them in the physical body; and on such rare occasions *the rendez-vous was made astrally by them*. They met me in the flesh at the time and place appointed beforehand. For my part I believe them to be human and living on this earth; but possessing terrible superhuman powers.

When such rendez-vous has been in a much frequented place there has been nothing in their personal appearance or dress to make them out as differing in any way from ordinary people except the appearance and sensation of transcendant health and vigour (whether they seemed persons in youth or age) which was their invariable accompaniment; in other words, the physical appearance which the possession of the Elixir of Life has traditionally been supposed to confer.

On the other hand when the rendez-vous has been in a place free from any access by the Outer World they have usually been in symbolic robes and insignia.

But my physical intercourse with them on these rare

occasions has shown me how difficult it is for a Mortal, even though advanced in Occultism, to support the presence of an Adept in the physical body.... I do not mean that in such rare cases of physical converse with them that the effect produced on me was that intense physical exhaustion which follows depletion of magnetism; but, on the contrary, the sensation was that of being in contact with so terrible a force that I can only compare it to the continued effect of that usually experienced momentarily by any person close to whom a flash of lightening passes during a violent storm; coupled with a difficulty in respiration similar to the half strangling effect produced by ether; and if such was the result produced on one as tested as I have been in Occult work, I cannot conceive a much less advanced Initiate being able to support such a strain, even for five minutes without death ensuing.

Almost the whole of the Second Order Knowledge has been obtained by me from them in various ways, by clairvoyance—by astral projection on their part and mine—by the table, by the ring and disc[4]—at times by Direct Voice audible to my external ears and those of the Vestigia[5]—at times copied from books brought before me, I knew not how —and which disappeared from my vision when the transcription was finished—at times by appointment *astrally* at a certain place, till then unknown to me; an appointment made in the same manner and kept in the same manner as in the case of those rare occasions when I have met them by appointment in the physical body.

The strain of such labour has been, as you can conceive enormous; in special, the obtaining of the Z ritual, which I thought would have killed me, or Vestigia or both, the nerve prostration after each reception being terrible from the strain

[4] These can best be described as mediaeval equivalents of the ouija board of modern spiritualism and the pendulum used in modern radiesthesia. A gold ring is suspended on a silken thread and its gyrations over the disc, on which are written the letters of the alphabet, indicate the answers to the questions asked by the Magician.

[5] Vestigia is short for Vestigia Nulla Retrorsum, the magical motto of Mathers' wife.

of testing the correctness of every passage thus communicated; the nerve prostration alluded to, being at the time accompanied by profuse cold perspirations, and by severe loss of blood from the nose, mouth and occasionally the ears.

You know the extreme and sustained attention, and critical judgment requisite to obtain any reliable and truthful answers through the Table or Ring and Disc. Add to all this the Ceremonies of Evocation, almost constant strife with opposing Demonic Forces endeavouring to stop the delivery and reception of the Wisdom; and the necessity of keeping the mind exalted towards the Higher Self....

It is interesting to note that Westcott later (1916) claimed that the materials on which Mathers based his Second Order rituals were derived from a Continental Adept, Frater Lux Tenebres. Various members of the Golden Dawn claimed that this Frater Lux e Tenebres was, in normal life, a Dr. Thiessen or Thilson of Liège. I have for long assumed that this alleged doctor was, in fact, one of Mathers' 'Astral Masters' and had no actual existence on the physical plane, but I am now fairly reliably informed that the name of Dr. Thilson was familiar in Belgian Martinist circles at around the turn of the century.

Additional Note Mabel Collins, the spiritualist-turned Theosophist (see page 41) had certain links with ritual magic of a probably sinister variety. She was at one time the mistress of 'Roslyn d'O Stephenson', who claimed to have been initiated into a magical order by Bulwer Lytton, to have had first-hand experience of African sorcery and to know the identity of Jack the Ripper. In a recent book Melvin Harris has put forward the theory that Stephenson was himself the Ripper and that his murders were blood sacrifices carried out for the purposes of Black Magic.

CHAPTER FIVE

Some Personalities

By the middle of the nineties the Golden Dawn was well established in Great Britain with a membership of over one hundred drawn from every class of Victorian Society; Frater Voto Vita Mea, for instance, the Imperator of the Bradford Temple, was a watchmaker living in comparatively humble circumstances. It is perhaps worth-while to briefly examine the backgrounds and personalities of some of the more prominent members of the Order, for by doing so it is easy to see the roots of the personality clashes that were later to be the cause of so much strife and bitterness.

On the Rev. A. F. A. Woodford and Dr. Woodman[1] I need waste little time, for the first died shortly after the establishment of the Order and the second died in 1891 before the foundation of the Second Order.

Dr. Wynn Westcott, known in the Order by his magical mottoes of Non Omnis Moriar and Sapere Aude, was born in 1848. He was an occult scholar of considerable distinction, had translated the Qabalistic *Book of Formation* and the *Chaldean Oracles of Zorcaster* into English, and combined a profound knowledge of magic, the early history of chess and the Enochian system of Dr. Dee, with the somewhat surprising occupation of Queen's Coroner for North-East London. Many years later Crowley stated that Westcott's interest in corpses was more than a medical one—that he had, in fact, dabbled in necro-

---

[1] Woodman was known in the Order as Frater Magna est Veritas. Woodford's magical motto is believed to have been Sit Lux et Lux Fuit; the curious thing is, however, that I have seen this motto on documents dated after Woodford's death—I can only presume that someone else took over this name.

47

mancy. Crowley's statement was, of course, utterly lacking in truth; he seems to have taken enormous delight in making libellous statements about Golden Dawn members and in his novel *Moonchild* all the Order's leading figures are grossly caricatured—Berridge appears as Dr. Balloch, a professional abortionist, A. E. Waite as Arthwait, an incredibly pedantic Black Magician (there is a splendid parody of Waite's literary style), and W. B. Yeats as Gates, an unwashed Irish poet with astonishingly unsavoury fingernails.

Westcott was a personal friend of Madame Blavatsky and while she lived there was a friendly alliance between the Eastern Section of the Theosophical Society and the Golden Dawn. He was also associated with the Christian mystics Anna Bonus Kingsford[2] and Edward Maitland, of the London Hermetic Society, the co-authors of *The Perfect Way*.

In about 1897, Westcott gave up all connection with the Golden Dawn, thus leaving Mathers in complete control. Exactly why he chose to do this is not certain; one story says that, owing to some papers having been found in a hansom-cab, his connection with the Golden Dawn came to the attention of the Home Secretary, who decided that Westcott must either resign from the Order or cease to be a Coroner.[3] It is possible, on the other hand, that he simply found Mathers such a difficult colleague, that he chose to concentrate his energies on the Societas Rosicruciana in Anglia of which he was by that time Supreme Magus.

G. S. L. Mathers was undoubtedly the most flamboyant of the founders. Born in 1854, the son of a London clerk, he was educated at Bedford Grammar School and subsequently lived in Bournemouth with his widowed mother. While still a very young man he immersed himself in occult studies, became a

[2] This woman cries out for a really satisfactory study; while the lurid form of her visions probably owes much to the fact that she was an ether addict their content is of considerable significance.

[3] If the Home Office did object to Westcott's activities it was probably because of the ridiculous allegation that he was, quite literally, a disciple of Satan, which was made in the French anti-masonic press. Even after Leo Taxil had withdrawn his spurious 'revelations' (April 1897) the clerical fanatics continued to attack Westcott as the supposed grey eminence who had bribed or threatened Taxil.

Freemason, and translated three of the most important books from the Latin of Knorr von Rosenroth's monumental *Kabbalah Denudata*. Shortly after this he produced an English version of the *Key of Solomon*, probably the most widespread of all the mediaeval grimoires.[4]

In 1890 he became the curator of the Horniman Museum, probably through the influence of Miss A. E. F. Horniman who had been a fellow-student of his wife at the Slade and was also a member of the Golden Dawn.

In 1894 he and his wife, who was French-born and a sister of Bergson the philosopher, moved to Paris. At first they received a generous allowance from Miss Horniman,[5] but this ceased after a bitter quarrel. Subsequently Mathers made a living by selling Turkish Railway shares on commission. This somewhat erratic source of income was supplemented by contributions made voluntarily by some members of the Golden Dawn.

The Ossianic romanticism of the Celtic revival of the nineties had always possessed a certain charm for Mathers and after his removal to Paris he gave full reign to these proclivities. His habit of wearing full Highland dress was inoffensive enough —like the pseudo-Assyrian dress of the occultist and artist Sar Peladan it brought a touch of colour into the somewhat bourgois drabness of the Third Republic—but the staider members of the Golden Dawn were greatly alarmed by his assumption of the title of Count MacGregor of Glenstrae. Mathers claimed that he was perfectly entitled to both the name MacGregor and the title of Count of Glenstrae. Mathers, he explained, was derived from the Gaelic 'Mo Athair', the posthumous one, and was one of the names assumed by members of the clan Mac-Gregor after its proscription, while the title had been conferred on his Jacobite great-grandfather in recognition of services to the French cause in India. At about the same time those who disliked Mathers began to spread the story that he claimed to be James IV of Scotland—not, as everyone thought, killed at

[4] See Appendix B—Mathers' *Editions of the Grimoires*.
[5] The only allowance was £449 a year; this sum is so curiously uneven that I can only assume that the number 449 had some personal or magical significance.

the Battle of Flodden, but an immortal adept. It is impossible to know whether Mathers ever made such a ludicrous claim, but it is undoubted that the story damaged his reputation and that much was made of it when he was cross-examined some fifteen years later when appearing as a defence witness in the case of Jones *v*. The Looking Glass:

'Is it a fact that your name is Samuel Liddell Mathers?'
—'Yes, or MacGregor Mathers.'
'Your original name was Samuel Liddell Mathers?'
—'Undoubtedly.'
'Did you subsequently assume the name of MacGregor?'
—'The name of MacGregor dates from 1603.'
'Your name was MacGregor in 1603?'
—'Yes, if you like to put it that way.'
'You have called yourself Count MacGregor of Glenstrae?'
—'Oh, yes!'
'You have called yourself the Chevalier MacGregor?'
—'No, you are confusing me with one of Crowley's aliases.'
'Have you ever suggested to anyone that you had any connection with King James IV of Scotland?'
—'I do not quite understand your question. Every Scotsman of ancient family must have some connection with King James IV.'
'Have you ever stated that King James IV of Scotland never died?'
—'Yes. That is a matter of common tradition among all occult bodies; Alan Cunningham wrote a novel based on this tradition.'
'Do you assert that King James IV is in existence today.'
—'I refuse to answer your question.'
'And that his existence today is embodied in yourself?'
—'Certainly not!'
'Do you claim that Cagliostro never died and that you are him?'
—'Certainly not, you are again confusing me with one of Crowley's aliases.'

Mathers combined his occultism with a vast knowledge of military history, tactics and strategy; he seems to have forseen a great European conflict many years before it actually broke out, and those who knew him well considered that his opinions on military matters were well worth a respectful hearing. His studies of generals and generalship seem, alas, to have heightened his autocratic tendencies already present in his own character and to have led to an often unjustified arrogance to, and contempt for, his subordinates within the Order.

Mathers was known to his fellow-initiates by the initials (S.R.M.D. and D.D.C.F.) of his magical names S' Rhioghail Mo Dhream (Royal is my Race) and Deo Duce Comite Ferro (With God as My Leader and the Sword as my Companion).

W. B. Yeats was among the earliest members of the Order; according to his own account he was initiated in May or June 1887, but as this was some months before the Golden Dawn received its charter from Germany it is clear that his memory had led him astray. The actual date of his initiation seems to have been March 1890. He took the name Festina Lente, but after he had attained the grade of Adeptus Minor he was known as Frater D.E.D.I.—Daemon est Deus Inversus, meaning the Devil is the reverse side of God. This motto, which Yeats took from the French occultist Eliphas Levi, has a rather diabolical air about it and it appears that Yeats was fascinated by Diabolism (which he seems to have pronounced Dyahbolism) at the time. Max Beerbohm wrote that Yeats 'had made a profound study of it and he evidently guessed that Beardsley ... was a confirmed worshipper in that line. So to Beardsley he talked, in deep vibrant tones, across the table, of the lore and of the rites of Diabolism.... I daresay that Beardsley ... knew all about Dyahbolism. Anyhow I could see that he, with that stony common-sense which always came upmost when anyone canvassed the fantastic in him, thought Dyahbolism rather silly. He was too polite not to go on saying at intervals, in his hard, quick voice, "Oh, really, how perfectly entrancing." '

Yeats brought many others into the Isis-Urania Temple, including his uncle and Florence Farr, the actress. The latter appears to have had a considerable talent for Ceremonial Magic, she rose rapidly in the Order and under her magical name of Sapientia Sapienti Dona Data became Praemonstratrix of the London Temple in 1894. Unlike some of her later successors in this office she not only studied the theory of Magic but practised the classical techniques of invocation and evocation. On May 13th, 1896, for example, she, with the assistance of Alan Bennett, Charles Rosher and Frederick Leigh Gardner, evoked the mercurial spirit Taphtharthareth to visible appearance—or so the four of them believed.

Dr. Edward Berridge, a well-known homoepathic physician, was another active member of Isis-Urania. His beliefs were curiously mixed and his intense personal loyalty to Mathers and that which he taught was only equalled by his devotion to the strange sexual-pneumatic philosophy of Thomas Lake Harris and the brotherhood of the New Life. It was Berridge's attempt to convert Miss Horniman (Soror Fortiter et Recte) to these latter doctrines that led to her quarrel with Mathers and her eventual expulsion from the Order. Berridge had sent her some pamphlets by Harris which she regarded as pornographic (today they would not raise an eyebrow if printed in *The Times*, except perhaps by the quaintness of their language) and she demanded an humiliating apology. This Berridge, anxious to avoid trouble, gave her; nevertheless he was annoyed by her prudery and jokingly told a fellow-initiate that he intended to construct a wax image of her and stick pins into it. Eventually report of this reached Miss Horniman and she wrathfully told Mathers that if he did not expel Berridge his allowance would be cut off. Mathers refused to accept this ultimatum and, after many accusations and counter-accusations, Miss Horniman was expelled from the Order in December 1896. Some twenty-seven members of the Inner Order had unsuccessfully petitioned Mathers not to expel Miss Horniman; I suspect that he used the petition to line his waste-paper basket.

Under the pseudonym of Respiro, Berridge wrote a series of articles for the *Unknown World*, an occult magazine published by A. E. Waite, another member of the Golden Dawn. Waite had originally been introduced to the Order by Berridge, but had resigned after taking some of the elemental grades. Two or three years later, however, Waite had rejoined on the advice of Robert Palmer Thomas (Frater Lucem Spero) who told him he was missing something of inestimable value. On his elevation to the grade of Adept Minor Waite took the name Sacramentum Regis. He remained suspicious of the Occult teachings of the Order, however, for at heart he was always a mystic rather than a magician as was his close friend M. W. Blackden (Frater Ma Wahanu Thesi).

Born in 1875 of Plymouth Brethren stock, Aleister Crowley had read, while still an undergraduate at Cambridge, a book by A. E. Waite and, inspired by some dark hints given in the introduction to this book, had written to Waite asking if there was a 'Secret Sanctuary' to which he could gain admittance. Waite had sent a kindly, if a little unhelpful, reply, urging the young aspirant to read Madame de Steiger's translation of an eighteenth-century mystical work *The Cloud on the Sanctuary*.

Crowley did this and also buried himself in the study of obscure qabalistic texts. While in Switzerland he met Julian Baker, a young chemist who also studied alchemy, who introduced him to George Cecil Jones, another occultist and alchemist. Both Baker and Jones were members of the Golden Dawn and they introduced the enthusiastic Crowley to the Order in 1898. It was this introduction that was eventually to be responsible for a considerable increase in the tensions and suspicions that had been building up in the British Temples since the resignation of Westcott and Mathers' attainment of the sole chieftainship of the Order.

CHAPTER SIX

Hierarchy

Before continuing with the strictly historical narrative it is advisable to examine, first, what the Golden Dawn initiates meant by 'Magic', second, what was the theoretical basis of their practices and, third, the hierarchic nature of the Order's grade structure; for without some understanding of these matters it is difficult to either comprehend the motives of such men as Mathers and Yeats, or to fully grasp the complexities of the later history.

Magic was defined by one initiate as 'the science and art of creating changes in consciousness'[1] and to this phrase should, perhaps, be added the words 'and entering into contact with non-human intelligences'.

The fundamental theoretical postulates of Western Magic are few in number. First comes a belief in a system of correspondences between the universe as a whole (the macrocosm) and the individual human being (the microcosm). This correspondence must, of course, be taken as crudely physical—rather is it an astro-mental relationship in which the soul of man is, to use the Golden Dawn phrase, a magical mirror of the universe. Thus any principle that exists in the cosmos also exists in man; the cosmic force that the ancients personified as Diana, for example, corresponds to the human reproductive instincts, while that same force in its evil and averse aspect, which the ancients personified as Hecate, corresponds to the human sicknesses of sterility and abortion. As a corollary of this theory it is believed that the trained occulists can either 'call down'

---

[1] Thus Magic produces the same psychedelic effects as, for example, LSD, but without the harmful physical effects.

into himself a cosmic force which he desires to tap or, alternatively, 'call up' that same cosmic force from the depths of his own being. The first process is invocation and should never result in physical, as distinct from psychological manifestation; the second is evocation in which the magician projects a 'spirit' (i.e. a factor in his own psychological make up) into his so-called Triangle of Art and which is supposed to result, if a proper material basis has been used in the rite, in a visible manifestation of the force evoked. Associated with this doctrine of the macrocosm and the microcosm is a belief in a system of classification which affirms that there is a definite relationship between colours, shapes, numbers etc. and the various spiritual factors that make up the universe. Thus, if the magician wishes to invoke the spiritual principle symbolised by the god Thoth he would draw his circle in various shades of orange, his lamps would be eight in number, his sacrament would be white wine and fish[2] etc.—for all these things are associated with Thoth.[3]

The next great principle of Western Magic is the belief that the properly trained human will is, quite literally, capable of anything. A quotation from the great seventeenth-century theologian Joseph Glanvill admirably summarises this doctrine:

'And the will therein lieth, which dieth not. Who knoweth the mysteries of the Will with its vigour? For God is but a great Will pervading all things by nature of its intentness. Man doth not yield himself to the angels nor to death utterly, save only through the weakness of his feeble will.'[4]

The motivating power, then, in all magical operations, is the trained will of the magician. All the adjuncts of Ceremonial Magic—lights, colours, circles, triangles, perfumes—are merely aids to concentrating the will of the magician into a blazing stream of pure energy.

The last fundamental belief of Western Magic is that there

[2] If he was one of those misguided persons who take a short cut to success by the use of drugs he would take mescalin.

[3] The complete Golden Dawn system of classification was published, together with a great deal of new material, by Aleister Crowley in his *Liber 777*.

[4] Compare MacGregor Mathers 'In the Adept death can only supervene when the Higher Will consenteth thereto, and herein is implied the whole Mystery of the Elixir of Life'.

are other planes than the physical (in the Golden Dawn they were often referred to, following Eliphas Levi, as the Astral Light[5]) and other intelligences than those in physical incarnation—Man is regarded as being half-way up the ladder of evolution, not at its top. Some, at least, of the Golden Dawn initiates seem to have regarded this last belief as not so much an objective fact but as a reasonable working hypothesis.[6]

Strictly speaking, of course, there was not one Order but three. These may be tabulated as follows:

FIRST ORDER

Grade	Numerical Symbol
Neophyte	$0° = 0°$
Zelator	$1° = 10°$
Theoricus	$2° = 9°$
Practicus	$3° = 8°$
Philosophus	$4° = 7°$

(The Link-Lord of the Paths of the Portal in the Vault of the Adepti.)

SECOND ORDER

Grade	Numerical Symbol
Zelator Adeptus Minor	
Theoricus Adeptus Minor	$5° = 6°$
Adeptus Major	$6° = 5°$
Adeptus Exemptus	$7° = 4°$

THIRD ORDER
(The Secret Chiefs)

Magister Templi	$8° = 3°$
Magus	$9° = 2°$
Ipsissimus	$10° = 1°$

[5] The Astral Light of Paracelsus, Levi and the Golden Dawn must not be equated with the 'astral plane' of the Theosophists. By the term 'Astral Light' Levi meant all planes above the dense physical except the abstract spiritual.

[6] Brodie-Innes summed up this point rather well: 'Whether the Gods, the Qlipothic forces or even the Secret Chiefs really exist is comparatively unimportant; the point is that the universe behaves as though they do. In a sense the whole philosophy of the practice of Magic is identical with the Pragmaticist (sic) position of Pierce the American philosopher.' (1917 lecture entitled 'The Philosophy of Magic'.)

The first of these Orders was that of the Golden Dawn, divided into five grades. The first, and unquestionably the most important of these, was that of Neophyte to which the candidate was inducted by means of a ritual that gave him not only a glimpse of the Light to be experienced in the future, but a key (albeit in an embryonic and undeveloped form), to the inner and hidden significance of the entire Order. Those entitled to speak on the matter claim that there is no part of the Neophyte ritual that is not of great occult significance. For example, there exists a Golden Dawn manuscript known as Z2 which applies the formulae of the Neophyte ritual to operations so apparently diverse as transformations, divination, and talismanic magic.

This Neophyte grade was not attributed to the qabalistic Tree of Life[7] and was therefore known as the $0° = 0°$ grade. Immediately after admission to the grade the Neophyte was given the first 'Knowledge Lecture'; this contained various Hermetic teachings together with instructions on the meditations he was to perform as part of his psycho-spiritual training. He was also given the rubric of the 'Qabalistic Cross and the Lesser Ritual of the Pentagram' that he might copy, learn and practice it—thus arriving at some dim comprehension of the way to come into contact with spiritual forces. Like the rest of the matters taught in the Neophyte grade there is far more to these rituals than appears on the surface. Certain aspects of them, in a more highly developed form, pertain to the Portal and Adeptus Minor grades. It may be said that the techniques taught are, in fact, capable of almost indefinite expansion. Israel Regardie has written two books, *The Middle Pillar* and *The Art of True Healing*, which are little more than amplifications of the Ritual of the Qabalistic Cross and the Lesser Pentagram.

The next four grades of the Order were attributed to the Elements:

The grade of Zelator, $1° = 10°$, corresponding to Earth and the Sephirah Malkuth (the Kingdom) on the Tree of Life;

---

[7] An illuminating introduction to the Tree is given in *The Golden Dawn— its Inner Teachings* by R. G. Torrens (Neville Spearman, 1970). For greater detail, Dion Fortune's *Mystical Qabalah* and Aleister Crowley's *777 Revised* are invaluable.

The grade of Theoricus, $2°=9°$, corresponding to Air and the Sephirah Yesod (the Foundation); The grade of Practicus, $3°=8°$, corresponding to Water and the Sephirah Hod (the Splendour); and The grade of Philosophus, $4°=7°$, corresponding to Fire and the Sephirah Netzach (Victory).

The purpose of the four Elemental grades was very different from the purpose of the Neophyte grade. The Neophyte ritual was designed to introduce the aspirant to a new life, symbolised by his or her adoption of a new name or 'magical motto', and to open his or her soul to the Light; thus in one sense it may be regarded as an objective initiation in which a link was formulated between the microcosm and the macrocosm, between the objective universe and the subjective universe of the aspirant. The Elemental rituals on the other hand were designed to equilibrate the Elements in the aura of the candidate and were thus subjective initiations, their results in some ways comparable to those of a Jungian depth-analysis.

Each of these grades had, of course, a corresponding meditation and Knowledge Lecture.

The last grade of the Golden Dawn proper was that of the Portal, not attributed to any of the Sephiroth but to Paroketh, the Temple Veil that separates the four lower Sephiroth on the Tree of Life from Tiphareth, the Christ centre—to which are attributed all Slain and Risen Gods. To this grade was attributed the fifth of the Elements, Akasha or Spirit, symbolised by the Winged Egg and the topmost point of the Pentagram.

The Portal ceremony gave the aspirant an introductory glimpse of the Second Order, that of the Roseae Rubeae et Aureae Crucis—the Red Rose and the Cross of Gold. A waiting period of nine months—the analogy to gestation is obvious—had to elapse between the candidate undergoing the Portal Ritual and his or her reception into the Second Order by means of the Adeptus Minor ritual. This waiting period was mainly occupied in certain works of an interior, psychotherapeutic nature; this work of self-analysis and self-synthesis was of great importance, for should the unbalanced neurotic candidate have undergone the ritual of the Adeptus Minor it would have led not to an initiation, but to psycho-spiritual destruction.

The first part of this interior psychological work is aptly described in the Knowledge Lecture pertaining to this grade:

> ... realising that we are indeed in a Path of Darkness groping for light, we must feel our way to an understanding of the meaning of Life—the reason for death.

To those who feel the call to make this effort, comes the Order with a series of pictures, symbolic of the growth of the soul to new life. The meditations given with each grade are designed to lead the mind towards ideas which will assist in self-knowledge—universal impersonal ideas which each must find in his own way—'the secrets which cannot be told save to those who know them already'.

The Aspirant is led to look backwards. First he must acknowledge his debt to evolution through which has been perfected the instrument wherein his mind works and gathers material. Then, through meditation he is led to see himself as not only self-conscious—as one who receives impressions—one who criticises and watches—one whose will is interfered with—one who is misunderstood—one to whom others are 'persons' or masks—but, standing outside himself, he now becomes one who endeavours to sense how his mask appears to others—sees himself as part of the consciousness of others, as one who impresses, one who is criticised and watched, one who interferes with the will of others, one who misunderstands.

He may recall periods in his life when his convictions were sure, his judgments harsh and unjust, his actions shameful, and view himself in that picture dispassionately as an entity operative in the give and take of life, something growing and as outside the category of blame as is the bitterness of unripe fruit.

As the knowledge of his place and relative importance in the universe matures, he will attain strength to be honest with himself—ashamed of nothing he finds in his mind—one watching the antics of his personality with tolerant amusement—yet always learning.

He will reflect on words, and the power of words. He will catch himself weaving them—twisting their meaning—deceiving himself and others with them. He will catch himself under obsession to them—he will see how they fix and make possible the recall of events and emotions, and with this knowledge he will become aware of how his words affect other people.

As he begins to realise the tremendous miracle of words, the magic both good and evil of human communion by words, he will begin to grasp why the Order reiterates the importance of silence. The true Magician must understand his tools and, in periods of silence, he must contemplate words as one of them.

As he thus traverses the long road to self-knowledge, and no longer has to do battle for and indulging wounded feelings in defence of a totally false idea of himself, he is led to meditation on the various symbols of the cross, and from this to contemplate the Crucified One, revealed to the West as Jesus of Nazareth.

The second part of this work consisted of the exercises of the Middle Pillar and the placing of the Tree of Life in the aura—these are the extensions of the Qabalistic Cross and the Lesser Pentagram ritual referred to earlier.[8] In many ways these exercises are analogous to the Kundalini Yoga of the Hindus, the microcosmic Sephiroth corresponding to the various chakras; there is one extremely important practical difference, however. In Kundalini Yoga the process is commenced in Yesod[9] and finished in Kether, while the Middle Pillar exercise is commenced in Kether and finished in Malkuth. In other words, the Eastern technique is designed to raise matter towards spirit while the Western technique is aimed at the incarnation of spirit in matter. It is just this, apparently minor difference, that makes oriental methods so unsuitable for most Westerners.

[8] These techniques are described in detail in *The Golden Dawn—its Inner Teachings* by R. G. Torrens (Neville Spearman, 1970).
[9] In the Kundalini Yoga, the *ojas* which is taken as being sent up the etheric equivalent of the spine (after the sleeping serpent has been aroused) is regarded as a subtle form of *bindhu*, semen.

It will be noted that I have referred to the Portal grade as being the last grade of the First Order; in fact there is some confusion on this point in the Order documents, some references seeming to imply that the Portal is the first grade of the Second Order, others that it is the last grade of the First Order. The seeming contradiction is easily explained when one considers the nature of Paroketh, the Veil of the Temple, to which the Portal grade is attributed.

Paroketh is an analogue, on a lower level of the Abyss, that vast consciousness that separates the Supernal Triad on the Tree of Life from the seven lower Sephiroth. In one sense the Exempt Adept who reaches the stage of crossing the Abyss ceases to exist. He becomes a handful of dust, a 'Babe of the Abyss', all the stereotyped reaction-patterns of his old personality-complex are dissolved. On a lower level this is what precisely happens to the candidate who reaches the Portal; his or her past achievements become valueless, the honours and knowledge acquired in the First Order cease to have any real significance, yet he or she has not yet been reborn into the Beauty of Tiphareth—like the coffin of Mahomet the candidate hangs suspended between heaven and earth.

The main magical work was not commenced until the aspirant had entered the R.R. et A.C. In the First Order the work performed (apart from the previously mentioned Qabalistic Cross and Lesser Pentagram ritual) consisted of Tattvic vision and divination by means of Geomancy and the Tarot.

The object of the Tattvic vision—the observation and comprehension of the various elemental Kingdoms—has been practised in the West since time began, for, except in highly developed forms it pertains to primitive psychicism; but the technique used in the Golden Dawn was derived from an Indian Tantric school.[10]

With the synthetic genius so typical of the Order, this system was closely integrated into the general structure of Western esotericism.

[10] One of the Order instructions, that 'On the Tattvas of the Eastern School', was little more than a precis of an early Theosophical work, *Nature's Finer Forces* by Rama Prasad. Certain aspects of this work seem to me to be debased and superstitious; but each must judge for himself.

I shall not waste space on giving a detailed account of the technique used, for there is an excellent description of it in W. E. Butler's book *The Magician*. It may be worth noting however, that the method of 'rising on the Planes' given by Aleister Crowley in his 'Liber O vel Manus et Saggitae' (originally published in the *Equinox* and reprinted in *Magick in Theory and Practice*) is, while in appearance different, at root identical with the Golden Dawn tattvic system.

The practice of Geomancy, a method of divination that is attributed to the Earth elementals, was peculiarly suited to the members of the First Order—for 'the Elemental grades quit not Malkuth'. That is to say, the grades attributed to Air, Water and Fire were not so much an entering into the Spheres of Yesod, Hod and Netzach, but rather an entering into their reflections in Malkuth, the Kingdom of Earth—those familiar with a coloured delineation of the Tree of Life will remember that Malkuth is divided into four sections, representing Earth of Earth, Water of Earth, Air of Earth and Fire of Earth.

The methods used for divination with the Tarot cards were the simple ones that have been described in A. E. Waite's *Pictorial Key to the Tarot*—a far more complicated method and, it may be added, one of much greater significance spiritually, was taught in the Second Order.

The whole point of the study of divination was, first, to familiarise the student with the symbols of Geomancy and the Tarot and to correlate them with the Tree of Life, and, second, to begin to develop in the aspirant that spiritual intuition which is of so much greater importance than mere psychicism in the Divine Theurgy that is the higher magic.

The Adeptus Minor ritual was one of great beauty and immense significance. Magnificent temple-furniture, sonorous language an exalted teaching and symbolism, all combined to produce an ineradicable effect on the properly-prepared candidate. Like all the great initiation rituals its core consisted of the symbolic slaying and resurrection of the candidate; this death and rebirth is the Great Initiation—nor is it always subjective, as we are reminded by the case of Thakur Haranath, whose body passed through the process of physiological death when under the influence of an influx of atmic force.

The purpose of the Adeptus Minor ceremony is splendidly conveyed in the following extract from the second point of the ritual:

> Buried with that Light in a mystical death, rising again in a mystical resurrection, cleansed and purified through Him, our master, O Brother of the Cross and The Rose. Like Him, O Adepts of the Ages have ye toiled. Like Him have ye suffered tribulation. Poverty, torture and death have ye passed through. They have been but the purification of the Gold.
>
> In the Alembic of thine heart through the athanor of affliction, seek thou the true Stone of the Wise.

The grade of Adeptus Minor was divided into two sub-grades, Zelator Adeptus Minor and Theoricus Adeptus Minor. An enormous amount of magical work had to be done by the Minor Adept; he had to pass examinations in no less than fourteen subjects including:

> Knowledge of the Ritual of the Twelve Gates in skrying and travelling in the Spirit Vision answering to the diagram of the Table and Shewbread.
>
> The combination of divers forces so as to reconcile their action in the same telesma or symbol.
>
> and Thorough elementary knowledge of the formulae of the awakening of the abodes by means of the play or raying of the chequers of the lesser angles of the Enochian squares.

Some idea of the scope of the magical work laid down for the Adeptus Minor (as distinct from his own original research) can be obtained from the following catalogue of manuscripts circulating among the Zelalatores Adepti Minores:

(a) General Orders and full curriculum of prescribed work.
(b) Full Pentagram Rituals.
(c) Full Hexagram Rituals.

(d) Instructions for construction and consecration of the Lotus Wand.

(e) Description of the Adepts' Rose Cross Lamen and the Ritual of its Consecration.

(f) Sigils from the Rose, being a description of the way in which the Sigils of Angels, Spirits etc., are derived from the Rose Cross Lamen.

(g) Description of Sword and Elemental Weapons with Consecration Ritual.

(h) Clavicula Tabularum Enochi.

(i) Notes on the Obligation of an Adeptus Minor.

(k) Consecration Ritual of the Vault of the Adepti.

(l) History of the Order by N.O.M. (Wynn Westcott).

(m) Hermes Vision together with Coloured Delineation of the Geometrical Figures of the Sephiroth.

(n, o, p, q, r) Complete Treatise on the Tarot with Star Maps and details of the Tree of Life projected in a Sphere.

(s) The Book of the Concourse of Forces.

(t) The Book of the Angelical Calls or Keys.

(u) Lecture on Man, the microcosm.

(v) Hodos Chamelionis, the Minutum Mundum, being a treatise on the colour-scales of the Tree of Life.

(x) The Egyptian God-forms as applied to the Enochian squares.

(y) Rosicrucian Chess.

(z) Symbolism of the Temple and Ritual of the Neophyte Grade.

The sub-grade of Theoricus Adeptus Minor was the highest in the Golden Dawn. The Chiefs claimed to be Exempt Adepts, but presumably these were honorary titles as this grade cannot be fully functional save in those no longer in incarnation. Regardie, in his *My Rosicrucian Adventure*, refers to the institution of an Adeptus Major Ritual in 1892. This is quite incorrect; as previously stated it was the Adeptus Minor Ritual that was introduced in that year. Regardie seems to have incorrectly assumed that the Vault of the Adepts had been in operation since the opening of the Isis-Urania Temple and was thus led into his error. It is true of course, that allegedly higher initiations were introduced into some of the later schismatic fraternities that had their origins in the Golden Dawn; but the original Order knew none of these things and was firmly convinced that initiations beyond Adeptus Minor were not conferred in any earthly Temple.

Beyond the Order of the R.R. et A.C. came the Third Order. The members of this—the Secret Chiefs—were considered to be the Great White Lodge of the Adepti, the 'Mahatmas' who had given Madame Blavatsky her mission. The nature of these Adepti is splendidly conveyed by the following passage from the *Secret Doctrine*:

> Alone a handful of primitive men—in whom the spark of Divine Wisdom burnt bright, and only strengthened in its intensity as it got dimmer and dimmer with every age in those who turned it to bad purposes—remained the elect custodians of the Mysteries revealed to mankind by the Divine Teachers. There were those among them, who remained in their Kumaric (divine purity) condition from the beginning; and tradition whispers, what the secret teachings affirm, that these elect were the germ of a Hierarchy; which never died since that period.

Additional Note The quotation from Glanvill (see page 55) is not to be found in any of the printed writings of that author, although it was attributed to him by Poe.

CHAPTER SEVEN

Revolt

By the end of 1899 the Adepti Minores of both the Isis-Urania Temple in London and the Amen-Ra Temple in Edinburgh had become extremely dissatisfied with the regime of Mathers, whose increasing autocracy and growing friendship with Frater Perdurabo (Aleister Crowley) caused them great concern. They were also anxious to make their own contacts with the Third Order instead of relying exclusively on the intermediacy of MacGregor Mathers. In addition to this, personal disagreements were continually arising in the Isis-Urania Temple—Florence Farr described them as an 'astral jar'—which seem to have been caused by tension between members of 'The Sphere', a secret Society within the Order, and the rest of the Adepti Minores.[1]

At the end of the year the London officials administered a deliberate rebuff to Mathers by refusing to initiate his friend Crowley as an Adept Minor, a grade to which he was formally entitled by reason of his successful completion of the course of work enjoined on members of the Outer Order, on the grounds of his moral turpitude. Crowley was refused details of the charges against him (in fact the London Adepti had heard that he was a homosexual) and he hurried off to Paris where Mathers displayed his complete disregard for the opinions of the Isis-Urania chiefs by initiating Crowley in the Ahathoor Temple

[1] A contributory factor may have been Florence Farr's own occasional tendencies to autocracy; she suspended one Frater because his manner of reciting the ritual did not meet with her approval—the poor man had to temporarily transfer himself to the Bradford Temple. It is good to know that he was ultimately forgiven, for Yorkshire did not particularly agree with him.

66

on January 16th, 1900.[2]

Crowley then made a leisurely return to London and applied to Miss Cracknell, the acting secretary of Isis-Urania, for those manuscripts to which he was now entitled. She told him that she would arrange for them to be sent to him in due course, and Crowley, after a brief visit to Cambridge, returned to Boleskine, his Scottish home, where he arrived on February 7th and began to prepare to undertake the operations of Abramelin Magic.

The London Adepti regarded Crowley's initiation as the last straw. Florence Farr, who had already expressed the opinion that the London Temple should be closed down, wrote to Mathers telling him that she wished to resign as his London representative, but was willing to carry on temporarily until a successor could be found. Mathers, suspicious that Wynn Westcott was secretly responsible for his troubles, replied on February 16th in terms that shocked and amazed the recipient of his letter.

... Now with regard to the Second Order, it would be with the very greatest regret, both from my personal regard for you as well as the occult standpoint, that I should receive your resignation as my Representative in the Second Order in London; but I cannot let you form a combination to make a schism therein with the idea of working secretly or avowedly under Sapere Aude under the mistaken impression that he received an Epitome of the Second Order work from G. H. Soror Dominabitur Astris.[3] For this forces me to tell you plainly (and understand me well, I can prove to the hilt every word I say here, and more) and were I confronted with S.A. I would say the same, though for the sake of the Order, and for the circumstances that it would mean so deadly a blow to S.A.'s reputation, I entreat you to keep this secret from the

[2] Many years later Crowley gave 20/2/1900 as the date of his initiation. This error was caused by a misreading of his own diary for that year—the actual date was definitely as I have given.

[3] The magical motto of Anna Sprengel—the lady whose address had been found in the cipher manuscripts and who had, in due course, signed the original warrant of the Isis-Urania Temple.

Order for the present, at least, though you are at perfect liberty to show him this if you think fit, after mature consideration.

He has NEVER been at any time either in personal or written communication with the Secret Chiefs of the (Third) Order, he having himself forged or procured to be forged the professed correspondence between him and them, and my tongue having been tied all these years by a previous Oath of Secrecy to him, demanded by him, from me, before showing me what he had done, or caused to be done, or both. You must comprehend from what little I say here the extreme gravity of such a matter, and again I ask you, for both his sake and that of the Order, not to force me to go further into the subject.

In spite of these statements Mathers certainly believed in the real existence of Anna Sprengel for he concluded his letter by stating (erroneously) that she was with him in Paris. The lady concerned was in fact Madame Horos, an unsavoury adventuress, who had picked up a certain amount of information about the Golden Dawn from some Americans (who had been initiated in the Ahathoor Temple) and who managed to temporarily convince Mathers that she was the real Anna Sprengel by repeating to him details of a private conversation he had with Madame Blavatsky many years before. It was not long before Mathers realised the nature of the fraud, and after stealing some of his property, she decamped to London where she carried out some peculiarly nasty pseudo-occult sexual rites in Gower Street and was ultimately sentenced to a period of penal servitude.[4]

Florence Farr considered her Chief's letter for some days and then wrote to Westcott requesting an explanation of and a reply to Mathers' charges. Westcott replied in a surprisingly mild tone; he denied the accuracy of the charge of forgery, but said he could not prove it to be false as his witnesses were dead.

By this time the London Adepti, who had been informed of

[4] The fake Golden Dawn concocted by this woman is dealt with in my ninth chapter.

the nature of Mathers' letter by its recipient had decided that the matter must be further investigated and to this end, on March 3rd, they elected a seven-strong committee which wrote to Frater S.R.M.D. asking for proof of his allegations.

Mathers sent an immediate and fierce reply—he declined to produce any proof, refused to acknowledge the London Committee, and pointed out that as Chief of the Second Order he was responsible to only the Third Order. He followed this up by dismissing Florence Farr from her position as his London Representative (March 23rd) to which the London Adepti responded by sending him a defiant message on the following day and calling a general meeting of the Second Order for March 29th. At this general meeting the Second Order voted, with only five exceptions,[5] to depose their Chief from his headship and to expel him from the Order.[6]

Mathers reacted to this by writing to the rebels, threatening them with a magical current of hostile will:

... I tell you plainly that were it possible to remove me from my place as Visible Head of our Order—the which cannot be without my consent, because of certain magical links—you would find nothing but disruption and trouble fall upon you until you had expiated so severe a Karma as that of opposing a current sent at the end of a century to regenerate a Planet. And for the first time since I have been connected with the Order I shall formulate my request to the Highest Chiefs for the Punitive current to be prepared to be directed against those who rebel, should they consider it advisable.

[5] The Five who remained loyal to Mathers were Frater Resurgam (Dr. Berridge), Frater Volo Noscere (G. C. Jones), Soror Perseverantia et Cura Quies (Mrs. Simpson), Soror Fidelis (Miss Elaine Simpson), and rather surprisingly, Frater Non Sine Numine (Col. Webber). With the exception of Webber and Berridge all these were personal friends of Crowley—although later Mrs. Simpson was to break with him on the grounds that he continually visited her daughter Elaine's bedroom while in his astral body. Crowley denied that he had done anything of the sort but expressed his gratitude to Mrs. Simpson for giving him the idea and took up the practice forthwith!

[6] According to another account Mathers was only deposed at this meeting and was not expelled until April 19th.

69

Meanwhile at the end of March, Soror Deo Date (Mrs. Dorothea Hunter, one of the Order's clairvoyants) who seems to have taken over the secretaryship of the Isis-Urania, had written to Crowley refusing him any manuscripts, telling him that Isis-Urania did not recognise his membership of the Second Order, and informing him of the expulsion of Mathers.

Crowley immediately sent a letter to Paris offering his services to Mathers, of whom he was at that date an almost fanatical disciple, and after a disturbed night's sleep, during which he dreamt of a woman-tapir on an island, departed to London in order to investigate the situation at first hand. He found little to cheer him; the Vault of the Adepts was locked against him and those Adepti to whom he managed to talk seemed either hostile or despondent—his old friend Julian Baker, for example, said that the Second Order had no obligation to a forger and could continue on its own, in any case the documents were all rot, particularly Z2! Soon, however, Crowley heard from Mathers that his services had been accepted and he hurried off to Paris, where he arrived on April 9th to confer with his Chief. He had already concocted a plan which, he felt sure, would bring the revolting members to their senses and, after a long talk, Mathers gave a substantial approval to Crowley's proposals. Some three days later Crowley was given detailed instructions on how to act in London, together with much magical advice. His orders included:

(a) Detailed lists of new chiefs for Isis-Urania—the loyal five were to be rewarded.
(b) Instructions to seize the premises of the Order and the Vault of the Adepts, using legal processes should these be required.
(c) The outline of a new warrant for the London Temple which Mathers, the only link with the Secret Chiefs, would sign in due course.
(d) Instructions to interview each Adept separately and ask various questions, the answers to which would decide whether that Adept was to be expelled from the Order or admitted to the reconstructed Isis-Urania Temple.

(e) Much magical advice on how to arrange the interviews so that they would be successful—for instance symbols of Saturn were to be over the door 'so that those who pass come under the terror of Saturn'.

(f) Methods of dealing with Madame Horos, the false Anna Sprengel, should she be encountered.

The arrival of Crowley in London, where he was regarded by the majority of the London Adepti as (in the words of W. B. Yeats) an unspeakable mad person, caused considerable alarm amongst the rebels and they resorted to an occult attack upon him which came very near to Black Magic. Yeats described this attack in a letter to his fellow-occultist and poet A.E. (George Russell). According to Yeats two or three of the Order's thaumaturgists called up one of Crowley's mistresses and told her to leave him and some two days later she agreed to go to Scotland Yard and give evidence of 'torture and mediaeval iniquity'.

Crowley's diary gives quite a different account of this magical attack—his Rose Cross whitened, his rubber mackintosh burst into flames, and 'In the morning I was very badly obsessed and entirely lost my temper utterly without reason or justification. Five times at least horses have bolted at the sight of me.'

Crowley seems to have decided that Frater De Profundis ad Lucem (F. L. Gardner) was responsible for these unpleasant experiences and attempted to evoke Typhon-Set against him—unsuccessfully apparently, for Gardner was none the worse for Crowley's efforts. As none of the rebels evinced the slightest desire to have an interview with Crowley he resolved on more direct methods and, having hired some chuckers-out at a public house in Leicester Square, seized the Vault. The Second Order seized it back again with the aid of the Metropolitan Police and, for good measure, managed to get one of Crowley's creditors to issue a writ against him. Crowley had had enough and retired from the struggle leaving the Second Order to its own devices.

Meanwhile, in Paris, Mathers had taken a large packet of dried peas and baptised each one by the magical name of one of the rebels. Then, by the formulae of the Great Enochian Tablet of Spirit, he evoked the forces of Beelzebub and Typhon-Set and, while shaking the peas in a sieve, called upon those mighty devils to fall upon his enemies so that they might fall upon and confound each other with quarrels and continual disturbance. If one could use the argument of *Post Hoc Propter Hoc* this was one of the most successful curses of all time, for as we shall see, almost immediately violent disagreements began to arise within the hitherto united ranks of the rebels.

CHAPTER EIGHT

Miss Horniman is Disturbed

Shortly after the Second Order's declaration of independence the Council which it had elected as a temporary government until such a time as a permanent constitution had been agreed upon, decided, at the suggestion of W. B. Yeats, to re-admit Miss Annie Horniman to membership and to appoint her as the Order's Scribe. This was almost certainly a mistake; Miss Horniman was obviously a difficult person to get on with, as shown by her irreverently-bestowed nickname of 'Pussy', and she seems to have been constitutionally incapable of dealing tactfully with her fellow initiates.

On taking up her position the new Scribe was shocked to discover that there were great irregularities in the record of admissions and examinations, and in the list of members. She was even more disturbed to find that since Florence Farr had taken over the chieftainship of Isis-Urania on April 1st, 1897 she had not enforced the system of examinations within the Order.

She quickly began to make efforts to complete and correct the records but in this, so she alleged, she met deliberate obstruction from Florence Farr who was by now the Moderator of the Council of the Order. Florence Farr replied that the difficulties experienced by Miss Horniman were entirely her own fault 'for instead of sending the Examination Book ... she wrote ... a separate letter for every item of information required'. In September 1900, said the angry Moderator, she had to 'look up the books on four separate occasions for information which anyone could have got from the Roll and an address book at one sitting.' Miss Horniman could not accept that she herself was in any way responsible for the difficulties that she was undergoing and attributed all her tribulations to the existence

73

of secret groups within the Order.

The existence of these secret societies within a secret society had been legalised by Mathers as far back as 1897. Both Frater Sub Spe (J. W. Brodie-Innes) of the Amen-Ra Temple and Florence Farr had subsequently formed groups and the group led by the latter had become much the largest after it had amalgamated with a group which had been led by Westcott until his withdrawal from the Order.

Florence Farr's society was known, as has previously been stated, as 'The Sphere', and its inner work consisted largely of attempts to get more advanced teaching from the Third Order by means of contacts on the astral plane. In addition to this each member of the group identified himself with a particular Sephirah of the Qabalistic Tree of Life and by means of a particular type of meditation attempted to build up a globular projection of the Tree within the collective aura of the group as an entity.[1]

When, at the beginning of 1901, Yeats returned from Ireland, he was approached by Annie Horniman and asked to try to take action against the groups in general and 'The Sphere' in particular. Yeats, whose ties with Miss Horniman were close and complicated by her financial patronage of his literary and dramatic work,[2] agreed to do this and he approached Florence Farr asking her to give details of the Sphere's formulae to all Theorici Adepti Minores and to invite all Theorici who wished to do so to join the group. She agreed to do this, but at the same time announced that she intended to ask the Council, at its next meeting on February 1st, 1901, to declare that small secret groups were in accordance with the magical tradition and valuable elements in the spiritual life of the Order. She further stated that she would ask the next general meeting of the Second Order to legalise and approve the existence of 'The Sphere' and similar societies.

At the Council's next meeting her resolution was passed by

[1] They also made efforts to carry out astral investigations of various aspects of the Order's symbolism—see Appendix C for examples of astral workings.

[2] Yeats was to some extent torn between the forces of Pluto (as god of money) and Eros, for Florence Farr had at one time been his mistress. (See also foot of page 203, Appendix C.

a large majority. Previously to this M. W. Blackden and R. Palmer Thomas had put forward the perfectly proper proposal that Miss Horniman should be joined by two other scrutineers for the purpose of counting the votes in the next election to the Council. At this Yeats exploded with unreasoning rage and, in spite of the fact that the motion was substantially modified in order to get a compromise solution, insisted that the mere putting forward of the resolution was an attempt to throw unwarranted suspicions on Miss Horniman, to whom he demanded the two proposers should make an unqualified apology. M. W. Blackden did so, presumably in the hope that this gesture would help to create a more peaceful atmosphere within the Order, but Palmer Thomas gave a flat refusal, to which Yeats responded by suspending him from acting as Sub-Imperator of Isis-Urania until such time as the required apology was given.

A little later Miss Horniman announced her intention of resigning as Scribe and Yeats circulated a letter to the entire body of Second Order Adepti denouncing the groups as a disruptive influence, defending his patron against Palmer Thomas' alleged imputations, and sneering that the latter had not even consecrated his implements—a reference to the four elemental weapons (pantacle, wand, cup and dagger) and the Lotus wand which all Adepti Minores were required to personally make and consecrate.

R. Palmer Thomas replied as follows:

Ma Wahanu[3] and I distinctly stated that our motion was impersonal and simply an effort to secure a ballot with which less exception could be taken in view of the fact that the Council was making a precedent. This however, was of no avail, V.H. Fra. D.E.D.I. insisting on the idea of suspicion, which was introduced on the Council by him and him alone. As a compromise, the motion was subsequently modified on condition that those able to attend the General meeting in March should be allowed to ballot in the ordinary way.

[3] The motto, supposedly Egyptian in origin, of Blackden. Blackden devoted a considerable amount of time to his Egyptological studies; he had a theory that some parts of the so called *Book of the Dead* were in fact an initiation ritual. He produced a version of some parts of the *Book of the Dead* which was eventually published by the Societas Rosicruciana in Anglia.

75

The following statements regarding myself have been made by V.H. Fra. D.E.D.I.:

(a) That I was solely responsible for Ma Wahanu's ballot proposal. This is incorrect.

(b) That my action caused V.H. Soror F. et R.[4] to decide on resignation. This is incorrect, as I understand that the Sor. in question had expressed this determination previously.

(c) That I have not consecrated my Implements. It is somewhat difficult to see what this has to do with the case, or how the information was obtained—but it is equally incorrect.

(d) That I relied for courage on some Hierarchy. I am really at a loss to understand what is meant by this but in seconding Ma Wahanu's resolution I am not aware that I relied on anything but the common sense of the Council.

As to the illegal attempt to deprive me of my position as Vice-Imperator I will only commend it to your consideration as a specimen of the kind of tyranny that we are endeavouring to render impossible in our Order. Personally I have no ambition whatever for either office or influence, though it has naturally been a great pleasure to me to find that the confidence of many of my Fratres and Sorores in me has been so great that offices have been conferred on me.

Lucem Spero's dignified statement was incorporated into a 'Statement of the Majority of the Council' issued to the Second Order. This contained, as the following extracts will show, a strong defence of the propriety of groups and equally strong attacks on Yeats and Miss Horniman:

Any experienced occultist will tell you that it is impossible for any large number of people to perform magic with effect, and in all ages secrecy has been an indispensable adjunct to such work. Thus small secret groups are supported by magical tradition ... we consider it necessary to the life of the Order that members should be encouraged to investigate freely; and use the knowledge already obtained as much as possible

[4] Miss Horniman.

as a basis for further development; and we consider that the oath of fraternity should protect members from the suspicion and criticism of those with whom they do not happen to be working at the time.

Those of us who belong to the Sphere group hereby deny ... that we wqrk formulae opposed to the Order teaching and method.

... Since last November Fortiter has literally persecuted persons she suspected of belonging to the Sphere group, by word of mouth and in written letters and lectures, endeavouring to prove that it is a disintegrating force. As it has worked for three years and its members are those active members who have, before and since the Revolution, spent and been spent in the service of the Order this accusation is, on the face of it, absurd.

... Fortiter has said that the group is responsible for the scandal she has made and for her suspicions. A would-be homicide might just as well plead that if his victim had not been born, he would not have attempted to kill him.

Fra. D.E.D.I. ... did you all much service during the Revolution as you know from your printed documents. Since then he has attended the Council meetings and we all bear him witness that he has talked at greater length than all the members put together. His position among us is due now to his long connection with the Order, the originality of his views on Occult subjects and the ability with which he expresses them, rather than on the thoroughness of his Order work and methods ... he has put himself forever beyond our sympathy by a recent flagrant piece of audacity before which the little tyrannies of our recent Parisian Chief pale. As Imperator he has, without attempting to consult either the Praemonstratrix or the Cancellaria, demanded the retirement of a Vice Chief of Isis-Urania Temple because they had a difference of opinion in Council.

In a desperate effort to gain supporters before the crucial General Meeting scheduled for February 26th, Yeats distributed two other letters and a pamphlet to the Second Order. While the pamphlet (*Is the Order of R.R. et A.C. to remain a Magical Order*) was soberly enough written, Yeats' letter of February 21st employed such extravagant and alarmist language, that it must have alienated the very support that it was designed to attract. Amongst other wild allegations this letter affirmed that the legalisation of groups would allow a group to hold, if it so wished, a Witches Sabbath at the door of the Tomb of Christian Rosy Cross!

At the General Meeting the following resolution, proposed by Blackden, was passed by a large majority:

> If the liberty and progress of individual members, and of this Order as a whole, is to be maintained—for progress without liberty is impossible—it is absolutely necessary that all members of the Second Order shall have the undisputed right to study and work at their mystical progress in whatsoever manner seems to them right according to their individual needs and conscience, and further it is absolutely necessary that they shall be at perfect liberty to combine, like-minded with like-minded, in groups or circles formed for the purpose of that study and progress, in such manner as seems to them right and fitting, and according to their consciences, and that without the risk of suffering from interference by any member of any grade whatever, or of any seniority whatever— and furthermore that this is in perfect accord with the spirit and tradition of our Order which is always to allow the largest liberty for the expansion of the individual, and has always discountenanced the interference of any and every member with the private affairs, whether mystical or otherwise of any other member.[5]

Previously to this the meeting had voted down amendments from Yeats and J. W. Brodie-Innes and subsequently R. Palmer Thomas was voted back into office as Sub-Imperator. Yeats immediately resigned his office of Imperator of Isis-Urania, although it was not until some time later that both he and Miss Horniman resigned from the Order itself.

[5] In view of the length of this sentence it is perhaps advisable to state that Henry James was not a member of the Order!

CHAPTER NINE

A Bogus Golden Dawn

In the autumn of 1901 the Golden Dawn received a great deal of unwelcome publicity as a result of the trial for rape of Theo Horos, husband of the false Anna Sprengel who had temporarily deceived Mathers some eighteen months before. Madame Horos herself was charged with aiding and abetting this same rape.

Mr. and Mrs. Horos were an unlikely looking couple—she was remarkably fat and he was remarkably thin—and they had equally unlikely backgrounds. The lady, according to her own account, was born in 1854 of a German father and a Spanish mother. She was a precocious child, and, in 1866, when she was only twelve years old, founded the American religious movement known as Koreshan Unity—or so, at least, she said. In 1871 she married a Mr. Messant, but this marriage seems only to have lasted a short time, for in 1879 she married General Dis de Bar—it would be interesting to know from whom he obtained his commission—whom she divorced 'in 1884 or 1885 in some Western state'. It is surprising that she was so vague about the date and place of her divorce, for the good General paid her alimony of no less than $14,000 a year! Unfortunately, however, this very considerable sum was either paid irregularly or was insufficient for her needs—how else can one explain the fact that in 1888 she served six months imprisonment for swindling a Mr. Luther Marsh out of his Madison Avenue house, while a little later she served two years imprisonment for larceny in the State of Illinois? She seems to have further supplemented her income by bogus mediumship; the 'Flaming Star', official organ of the Koreshan Unity movement, described her as 'Dis

Debar a convicted spiritualist swindler' and said that she was 'the slickest and most accomplished crook-swindler ever known' —like the rest of the members of Koreshan Unity the writer seems to have been unaware that Madame Horos had founded the movement.

'Theo. Horos', whose real name was Frank Jackson, had met his future wife in 1898. He had been a member of Koreshan Unity and, indeed, had eventually become its Treasurer, but had had to resign from this position after meeting with some difficulties in attempting to balance his books.

It seems likely that the Rev. A. H. Becker, the Evangelical Pastor who officiated at the wedding of the pair, was impressed by the importance of his clients; for the Marriage Certificate reads:

> This certifies that Mr. Frank D. Jackson of Pontdulac, State of Wisconsin, and Princess Edith Loleta, Baroness Rosenthal, Countess of Landsfeldt, of Florence, Italy, were by me united in Holy Matrimony, according to the Laws of God and the ordinances of the State of Louisiana, at New Orleans, on the 13th day of November, in the year of Our Lord 1898.

Eleven months later the happy couple were living in Glen Echo, a Washington suburb, and here they were fortunate enough to make the acquaintance of a widow, a physician named Mary Evelyn Adams, usually known as Dr. Rose Adams.

In Rose Madame Horos and her husband seem to have found an easy victim. Madame Horos said that she and Theo had been appointed to do God's work—Theo was, in fact, a new incarnation of Jesus Christ while she, the Swami (as Madame Horos now called herself) was none other than the Mother of God! The theology of Theocratic Unity—for so the Swami and her husband called their new movement—was a complicated one; not only was Theo the Christ but he was also, in some mysterious way, a Mother-God, and although he was temporarily confined in a male body, he would some day dematerialise and reappear as a gloriously beautiful woman.

The prospect of this unlikely event seems to have pleased and excited Rose Adams for, after having read the Sermon on the Mount and heard Madame Horos quote the twelfth chapter of Revelations and the ninth verse of the third chapter of the Epistle of St. John, she hurried off to the Washington Savings Bank where she withdrew all her money and handed it to Theo. After this act of sacrifice she was treated, to use her own words, as a perfect slave.

Late in 1899 Mr. and Mrs. Horos, accompanied by Rose Adams and other members of Theocratic Unity, set off for Europe. After a quick and fruitless stay in London they hastened on to Paris where, as was mentioned in my seventh chapter, they met Mathers.

Mathers described his relationship with the pair in the following letter to the Spiritualist magazine *Light*:

Order of the G.D. and the Horos Case

Sir,

I am, and have been for years, the Head of the above Order, which counts as its members all over the world, persons not only of strict integrity and moral worth, but also in many cases of the highest social and intellectual rank. In justice to it and them, I wrote on October 13th to Mr. Curtis-Bennett to protest against the shameful and utterly unauthorised use of its name for their own abominable and immoral purposes by the execrable couple calling themselves 'Mr. and Mrs. Horos'. In case that letter should not be read in court, I will ask you to insert this in the columns of your valuable journal.

The teachings of this Order of the G.D., which has existed from ancient time, inculcate nothing but the highest social and religious virtues, moral purity, and fraternal charity; and those persons who cannot adhere to these principles are neither allowed to become nor to remain members.

Among its principal objects of study are Archaeology, Mystical Philosophy, and the origin and application of Religious and Occult Symbolism. It teaches respect for the truths of all religions, as well as for the religious feelings and ideals of our neighbours. Its real title has from ancient time been kept secret, to prevent, as far as possible, imposters and adventurers from making use of its name to shield their malpractices.

Coincident with certain dissensions in my Order, stirred up by a few members, constant fomenters of discord, jealous of my authority, though clamorous for my teaching, the so-called Mr. and Mrs. Horos and a Mrs. Rose Adams, who said she was a Doctor of Medicine, came to me in Paris in the beginning of last year (1900), with an introduction from an acquaintance of good social standing. At this time my name was well-known here in connection with lectures on Ancient Egyptian Religious Ceremonies. The female prisoner stated that they had come with the intention of aiding me in this, and she professed to be an influential member of the Theosophical Society, and also of my own Order, giving me the secret name of a person of high occult rank in it, who had been reported to be dead some years before. I have yet to learn how, when, where, and from whom, she obtained the knowledge of that Order which she then certainly possessed. She was also acquainted with the names and addresses of several of the members, notably of those belonging to the discordant category. Under these circumstances she managed to take from my house (besides other things) several manuscripts relating to the Order of the G.D., which she promised to return, but which I have not succeeded in getting back from her. From these she and her infamous accomplice would seem to have concocted some form of initiation under the name of my Order, to impose upon their unfortunate victims. It did not take me long to find out the kind of persons the so-called Mr. and Mrs. Horos were, and I refused to receive them; but as Head of my Order I did not want to lose touch of them entirely till I could find out more about them, and especially whether they were emissaries of enemies within my Order, or of those without, or of both.

They soon quitted Paris for London, and again coincident with their presence more dissension arose in my Order there, culminating in severance of the discordant members from it.

In January last one of these ex-members (who was evidently then in touch with the prisoners indirectly) wrote

to me concerning them; and notwithstanding the circumstances existing between him and me, I sent him a letter of
warning.

Shortly after this another of these ex-members boasted
openly that he had unmasked the prisoners and forced them
to abandon their operations in London, but, unfortunately,
in view of the appalling evidence that has just been given
before the magistrate, that boast was both premature and
idle.

Apologising for trespassing, so long on your valuable
space, and thanking you for inserting this letter, believe me,
Sir,

Faithfully yours,

G.S.L. MacGregor-Mathers

(Comte MacGregor de Glenstrae.)

28 Rue Saint Vincent, 28,
Paris, October 23rd, 1901.

My name is well-known as a student of Occultism,
Archaeology, and Egyptology.

As the case had been *sub judice* from October 12th, 1901
until the following December 20th *Light* did not publish this
letter until January 1902.

While in Paris Madame Horos—now calling herself Swami
Viva Ananda—had some correspondence with W. T. Stead, no
longer the same man whose *Pall Mall Gazette* had shaken
Victorian England with its Crusade against childhood prosti-
tution, but an ageing and, it must be admitted, slightly ga-ga
spiritualist. Although he did not accede to the Swami's request
that *Borderland*, Stead's spiritualist magazine which had
recently ceased publication, should be resumed under her
control, he seems to have taken her much more seriously than
she deserved. We find him writing to her on February 16th,
1900: 'I am glad to know that you are finding the work on the
Continent is prospering. I hope that your civic theosophic
centre will be a Pharos from which light may stream over a
darkened Continent. Good citizenship, free from sectarian or
national limitations, in France is rare indeed. You have a great

work in hand, and I do not think you need so much to exert yourself to visualise the awful consequences of the neglect of moral principle. They are visible enough to all of us. What you need to do is to make visible and real before the eyes of mankind the better social order that would result from the adoption of sounder principles in social and political life. I presume that my double[1] has not visited you again, as otherwise I am sure that you would have told me.'

In spite of Stead's encouragement Mr. and Mrs. Horos seem to have had no success in their attempts to 'spread light over a darkened Continent', and, after a brief return to London, they sailed for South Africa on April 12th, 1900 accompanied, as usual, by Rose Adams. Once in Cape Town they set up a bogus occult establishment, dealing in almost every sort of quackery, which appears, for a time at any rate, to have thrived; they even got some favourable publicity in a local newspaper:

Occult Science in Cape Town. Readers of the fascinating *Caves and Jungles of Hindostan*, *Isis Unveiled*, and other works of the late Madame Helena Petrovna Blavatsky, and those who do not despise the labours of Paracelsus and Raymond Lully will be interested to hear that a school of occult science has recently been established in Cape Town by Madame Swami Viva Ananda and a staff of competent assistants. Madame Ananda (who has adopted the professional title of Madame Helena) is a qualified lady doctor who, believing the spirit greater than the body, has laid aside all medicine and trusts solely to faith and the power of the spirit to cure her patients. As the fame of Madame's reputed cures has already extended to country districts a *News* representative visited her establishment in Bree-street a few days ago and was courteously shown round by Madame Helena herself and her husband, Mr. Theo. Horos. The treatment room is a fair-sized chamber in the rear of the house containing several beds... and the treatment is confined to massage and magnetic movements. Up to the present about

[1] One can only presume that Madame Horos had told Stead that, unknown to his conscious mind, he had visited her in his astral body!

50 patients have been or are receiving benefit from the treatment. But Madame Helena does not confine herself to medical science alone; she claims, as Madame Blavatsky, her friend and co-worker, claimed, to be in communion with the spirit world, to have been educated amongst the Mahatmas; and to be throughly proficient in what is vulgarly known as palmistry and clairvoyance, but what has also been described as psychic philosophy. The genuineness of her experiments has been attested by several well-known citizens of Cape Town, and her powers have been successfully appealed to in several private detective cases. Madame receives her numerous clients in her salon, which is a modest little room remarkable only for several large unframed pictures on the wall. One of these represents Madame herself reclining on a living tiger, near the Temple of the Unknown, where she claims to have been initiated. Madame herself is an imposing presence, and is conversant with all subjects touching her work. She makes no mystery of her claims, but gives them the widest publicity, and in her weekly lectures, which are held every Sunday afternoon, challenges full inquiry. Palmistry, the most elementary science which she professes, she claims to be an exact science, to a certain extent dependent on accurate mathematical combination. Beyond that she admits the necessity of calling into aid her psychic and thaumaturgic powers. In short, Madame Helena puts forward claims which she contends are in complete accordance with Biblical texts and testimony. She makes many statements which to the ordinary individual savour of black magic, but above all she vigorously preaches the religion of charity in its widest sense. No poor man, she says, need apply to her in vain for aid, for all her skill and experience are at his service, provided he be really poor. Already a dozen pupils have enrolled themselves in the school, and it seems probable that Madame's stay in Cape Town will not be short as she has already won a large circle of those who, like her friend Mr. W. T. Stead, take an interest 'in those things which lie on the borderland of the natural and the celestial worlds.'

Inevitably, this happy state of affairs did not last for long; complaints were made to the police and, hearing that a warrant for their arrest was about to be issued, the Swami and her husband returned to London where they arrived in the late spring of 1901. Their first thought was to find some way of raising money—as usual there was no sign of General Dis de Bar's alimony, nor did Theo seem to derive any benefit from the 7,280 acres of American agricultural and timber land that he said he owned.

They seem to have thought of opening a 'diploma mill'—a fake academic institution selling fake degrees—and they had imposing certificates, printed:—'College of Occult Sciences: This certifies that...................of.........................., having presented as student of the College of Occult Sciences, and having passed a satisfactory examination in all branches, is entitled to receive the degree of 'Swami', and is hereby authorised as a graduate in mental therapeutics and psycho-pathology of the College of Occult Sciences located in Cape Town, South Africa, to treat and teach all the subtle occult laws, which embrace anthropo-magneto-electro-psycho-pathy, osteopathy and massage. This certifies that this graduate is duly qualified to form classes under the high and mighty title of 'Swami' for spiritual and mental unfoldment. Given under our hands and seal this......................'

This idea does not seem to have been proceeded with, possibly because of excessive American competition, and, instead, Mr. and Mrs. Horos decided to (a) attract as many people into their orbit as possible, (b) put these people through fake Golden Dawn initiations (they still had the manuscripts stolen from Mathers) and (c) obtain every penny they could from the people in question.

In Edwardian England it was often difficult for marriageable men and women of the lower middle classes to meet each other socially. Consequently, advertisements inserted by those inclined to matrimony were a common feature of the popular press. Theo and his wife decided that advertisements of this type were a good method of obtaining both new recruits for their 'Theocratic Unity', and money for themselves. Soon advertisements were placed in suitable papers; the following from the *People* of July 14th, 1901 is typical: 'Foreign gentleman, 35, educated, attractive, of independent means, desires to meet a lady of means with view to matrimony.'

The experiences of the women who answered these advertisements was markedly similar, and it is thus clear that the Horos couple did not act on impulse in their dealings with these same women, but rather in accordance with a carefully pre-arranged plan. Let us examine a typical case, that of Evaline Mary Maud Croysdale, commonly known as Vera.

Living in Hull, with her guardian, Vera saw and replied to one of Theo's advertisements. Soon came an enthusiastic answer; Theo, himself a wealthy man, was travelling the world with his even wealthier mother. Would Vera, could Vera, come and stay with mother for a few days or a week? At first she hesitated, but then Theo wrote again—his mother was clever, beautiful, brilliant and, best of all, had 'great powers of reading the inner soul'. This was irresistible and Vera hastened off to Clapham that she might meet this paragon of all the virtues.

Theo's mother, in reality Madame Horos, greeted her prospective daughter-in-law with a kiss. Then, after many questions about family, friends, and financial affairs, mother produced a large painting of herself riding, in a reclining position, on a tiger. This same painting was to be the source of much hilarity when produced in Court some three months later.

Shortly afterwards Theo arrived and, after presenting Vera with a thornless red rose, told her that her troubles were now all gone. Vera was delighted with all this; later, in Court, she rather ambiguously gave her age as 'about 23' and one is inclined to suspect that she wanted a husband rather badly.

If so, she got her desire a few days later, for Theo 'married' her by a simple ceremony of his own devising—that is to say, he got into bed with her, muttered some words that he said were vows, informed her that they were now married according to the rites of the Golden Dawn, and proceeded to consummate the marriage. Vera would have preferred a more orthodox type of marriage and was somewhat worried by the incident,

87

but Theo assured her that his saintly mother, the soul-reading Swami, both knew and approved of his action. At first Vera must have found this difficult to believe but, no doubt, she was convinced of its truth when Madame Horos took to joining them in bed and lying by their side as they had sexual intercourse.

A little before this, Vera had been 'initiated', by the Horos couple, into what, she thought, was called the Hermetic Order of the Golden Door. From Vera's description of the ceremony it is certain that the Golden Dawn Neophyte Ritual was used —it probably puzzled her a great deal as she was not a clever girl.

The household were now living at 99 Gower Street, later to be the offices of the *Spectator*, and money began to run short; fortunately Vera had some diamond ear-rings, a diamond pendant, and other simple jewels. These she 'lent' to Theo for pawning—he was supposed to redeem them the next Tuesday, but never did. On another occasion he took away her gold brooch and pawned it for thirty shillings of which he munificently gave her twelve. With this sum she set off on a cycle tour, joining friends in the West Country.

I am sure that either Madame Horos or her husband— perhaps both of them—had considerable hypnotic powers. For on what hypothesis, other than post-hypnotic suggestion, can one explain the fact that after she had joined her friends this deluded and defrauded girl wrote the following letter to her 'Swami'?

Yeovil

My Own Dearest Mother,

Have arrived, so far, safe and sound. Am now going to be busy eating my lunch. Dora and all my friends were at the station to meet me, and all gave me a very hearty welcome. We are a very lively party, and all seem intent on enjoying ourselves. Love to all. Much love and heaps of kisses for yourself.

Ever Your Loving Daughter,
Vera

It was not, however, for obtaining Vera Croysdale's trinkets by means of a fraudulent promise of marriage that Theo was sentenced to fifteen years' penal servitude and his wife to a similar sentence of seven years; it was for the rape of a sixteen-year-old Birkenhead girl named Daisy Pollex Adams.

Daisy, later described in court as a 'pretty little thing' had a respectable lower middle-class background; her father was a Master Mariner while her mother had been a Police Court Missionary, a grim Victorian ancestor of the modern Probation Officer. Mrs. Adams was a member of a small religious sect, called the Army of the Lord, in which she was known as Sister Miriam. The leader of this sect was a Mr. Wood of Brighton; there were many odd people who flourished in the religious underworld of late Victorian and Edwardian England but, I think Mr. Wood was the oddest of them all. He believed that in a former incarnation he had been King Solomon, and by this name he was known to his followers. He was much concerned about the correct translation of the Hebrew words Tohu and Bohu and for a time, at least, he believed that Madame Horos was the Queen of Sheba, he called his house 'Arregosobah' and, strangest of all, he believed that a diet of freshly mown grass supplemented with a mixture of chalk and water was completely sufficient for all the needs of the human metabolism.

For a time Mr. Wood was very impressed by 'Theocratic Unity'—later he was to change his mind and decide that an obscure text in the Book of Daniel implied that the movement should be 'abolished and destroyed'—and it was at his home, in April 1901, that Mrs. Adams enjoyed her first brief meeting with Theo and the 'Swami'. She re-met them on the night of the following August 20th when they came to stay at her home in Birkenhead which they were visiting for the purpose of giving a lecture on diet—both were great advocates of a strictly vegetarian diet, although themselves indulging in both beef and beer.

On the following day one of the couple suggested to Mrs. Adams that Daisy and her fourteen-year-old brother should return with them to London 'in order to complete their education'. Daisy was to be taught shorthand, typing, music, drawing and painting, while the boy was to be taught singing at St. Paul's Cathedral. The children's mother agreed to this attractive proposal and, on August 22nd, Mr. and Mrs. Horos took the children to London where, almost immediately on arrival, they were subjected to a lecture on the virtues of fruit, nuts and water.

On the following day they left London for a short visit to Brighton. Later that day Theo told Daisy that she was to spend the night in his bed; this was essential, he said, for him to privately expound certain secret teachings of the Golden Dawn to her. In due course they retired for the night where, after being informed by Theo that the Spirit of Christ was in him and that she was to be his 'little wife', Daisy was initiated into the practice of mutual masturbation. A few days later full sexual intercourse took place with, admittedly, the consent of Daisy who, as she was later to tell the Court, was under the impression that Theo was the Son of God and could do no wrong.

On Tuesday, August 27th, Daisy was 'initiated' into the bogus 'Golden Dawn'. From the Solicitor-General's description of this 'initiation' it is clear that, once again, Mathers' Neophyte Ritual was used:

There was a throne erected, on which Theo sat as a kind of high priest. At the other end of the room there was another throne on which the 'Swami' sat—each of them dressed in fantastic costumes symbolical, he supposed, of the higher life they were leading. An altar was set up on the room, on which was a red cross; a wine and a water vessel, occult signs, lamps here and there; and were a number of other officers or priests of the order present all decorated in their own peculiar way according to the particular office they held. When all was ready the candidate for initiation (Daisy) was blindfolded outside the room and rope placed around the body, and she was led to the door of the hall for admittance. She was met at the door, and then an act of purification was performed, and the hall was purified. The candidate was taken three times round the hall, and was presented first at the throne of darkness and then at the throne of light, and was next brought before the altar and her hands placed on the red cross and the triangle. In that solemn way she was made to repeat the oath of obligation of secrecy.... Then the bandage was removed from the candidate's eyes and she found herself standing with a sword poised above her head, and the benediction was pronounced.

The oath referred to was the Golden Dawn's neophyte oath and was read out in full and later printed in several newspapers much to the embarrassment of the members of the genuine Golden Dawn.

On August 30th, 1901 the 'Theocratic Unity' was expelled from its hired rooms at 99 Gower Street by the landlady, a Mrs. Annie Lewis, who described herself as a 'mental healer' and an expert on 'mental therapeutics'. Three months later, at a time when to admit having been associated in any way with Madame Horos was to court considerable unpopularity, Mrs. Lewis claimed that she got rid of her boarders because she could not agree with their teachings and was disgusted by the fact that, while themselves being great meat-eaters, they continually and enthusiastically preached vegetarianism to others. It is probably significant, however, that Mr. and Mrs. Horos were greatly in arrears with their rent when they left Gower Street; no doubt Mrs. Lewis simply wanted more reliable tenants.

Some of the members of the 'Theocratic Unity' moved to Park Street. Others, including the leaders, moved to Gloucester Crescent. It was here, on September 18th, that Theo, with the assistance of his wife, raped Daisy, who by now seems to have begun to doubt his semi-divinity and resisted his advances.

Laura Faulkner, a newcomer to the menage—she had been brought in by a matrimonial advertisement published in the *People* of September 8th—stated in Court that she had been instructed, on the morning of the eighteenth, to bring Daisy to the 'Swami's' bedroom; this she did, and subsequently heard the girl crying out 'Oh! Theo, don't'. Later she saw Daisy leave the bedroom, her eyes swollen and red with weeping, and within an hour Daisy had told her and Olga (another would-be wife of Theo who had been swindled out of £53 and some fish-knives and forks) that she had been raped, saying 'You don't know the treatment I have received this morning. The Swami held me by the head.'

Later that same day the police arrested Madame Horos on a charge of theft but, owing to a lack of evidence, she was discharged by the magistrate. At this point a Mr. Renzi, who had also lodged at Gower Street, wrote to Daisy's father urging him to remove his children from their poisonous environment; this letter temporarily alarmed Mrs. Adams, but her fears were allayed when shown a letter that Theo had somehow induced Daisy to write. In this letter Daisy stated that 'she was sorry she had wronged Theo and would vow on her knees before God to remain true to him and the Swami even if she was tortured to death.'

Time was running out for Theo and his 'Swami', however, and they were arrested on September 26th—astonishingly enough at the Birkenhead home of Daisy's mother, who had managed to cling to the belief in the purity of their ideals, surely a considerable tribute to the powers of persuasion of Mr. and Mrs. Horos.

On December 20th, 1901, Mr. Justice Bigham, after stating that it was difficult to conceive of more revolting or abominable conduct than that of the prisoners, sentenced Theo to fifteen years' penal servitude and the 'swami' to seven years—she, at least, retained her spirit to the end, contending against all the evidence, that Theo was incapable of sexual intercourse, giving forth dark intimations of sinister plots against her 'mission', and being very rude indeed to the Solicitor-General.

It may be thought that I have devoted an excessive amount of space to people who were, after all, only two rather seedy sexual perverts and confidence tricksters having only a tenuous connection with Ritual Magic and the Golden Dawn. I do not think that such a conclusion would be justified for, in my opinion, the Horos case had a considerable negative importance—it had a damaging effect on the Order. The ordinary members were, to some extent at least, demoralised; they were upset at having the obligation they had made as Neophytes printed in the popular press, they were annoyed by the Solicitor-General who had described their Neophyte ritual as being 'most blasphemous', and—perhaps this was worst of all—they realised that those members of the public who had read the case with sufficient attention to differentiate between the real Golden Dawn and its imitation regarded them, not as the Great Adepts they considered themselves to be, but as a set of amiable lunatics.

Many members left the Order at around this time[2]—I am confident that this was because of the impact of the Horos case.

The Horos case did have one permanent effect on the Order; the penalty clauses of the Neophyte oath, which had been subjected to such strong criticism in the press, were henceforth modified and toned down. Before the case the relevant passage had read: 'All these points I generally and severally upon this sacred and sublime symbol swear to observe without evasion, equivocation, or mental reservation of any kind whatsoever, under the no less penalty on the violation of any of them than that of being expelled from this Order as a wilfully perjured wretch void of all moral worth and unfit for the society of all upright and true persons, and, in addition, under the awful penalty of voluntarily submitting myself to a deadly and hostile Current of Will set in motion by the Chiefs of the Order by which I should fall slain or paralysed without visible weapon, as if blasted by the Lightening Flash.' The amended version reads: 'I swear upon this holy symbol to observe all these things without evasion, equivocation or mental reservation, under the penalty of being expelled from this Order for my perjury and offence, and furthermore submitting myself to the Divine Guardians of this Order living in the Light of their Perfect Justice. They journey as upon the winds, they strike where no man strikes, they slay where no man slays.'

---

[2] I suspect, but cannot prove to my own satisfaction, that F. L. Gardner was one of these.

CHAPTER TEN

Splinters

With the withdrawal into inactivity of W. B. Yeats and Annie
Horniman the Second Order was free to turn its attention to
the problem of the future government of itself and the dependent Outer Order.

To this end the members of the R.R. et R.C. authorised a
Committee of Three to temporarily govern the Order and to
draw up a suggested constitution which would be submitted
to the Second Order for approval at the next annual general
meeting. At first this executive group consisted of P. W.
Bullock, M. W. Blackden and J. W. Brodie-Innes, but after
a short time Bullock resigned and his place was taken by Frater
Finem Respice—Dr. R. W. Felkin, a distinguished physician
and one of the pioneers of scientific tropical medicine.

As the year drew on it became clear that the Committee was
unlikely to have its draft constitution ready for discussion at
the end of the year, and a group of members, led by A. E.
Waite, drew up their own involved proposals. These were presented in all their complexity to the next General Meeting,
but as the Committee of Three opposed them—although,
according to Waite, M. W. Blackden had given them his secret
approval—they were voted down. The Committee assured the
Second Order that the draft would be ready shortly and consequently the same three Adepti were re-elected to office for
another year.

Early in 1903 the triad submitted the proposed scheme of
government to a General Meeting held at Mark Masons' Hall.
A. E. Waite, who seems to have desired nothing but to get the
Order into his own hands, proposed several amendments with

94

the object of securing a rejection of the constitution, but to his surprise and alarm Brodie-Innes and his colleagues accepted them and modified their proposals accordingly. Waite, who loathed Brodie-Innes and was anxious to isolate him, then urged the Adepti to vote against the constitution as a whole. Although only a minority of the Order followed Waite in this course of action there were sufficient of them to ensure that the new constitution did not get the required two-thirds majority. Waite followed up his success by speaking, as always, at considerable length; he said that the Third Order was non-existent, that the Order's rituals needed much revision, and that the magical tradition should be abandoned as illusory and a dangerous path, leading only to the Abyss. He concluded, by announcing that he had no use for the Order in its present form, and inviting all those who agreed with him that the Golden Dawn should abandon Ritual Magic and all astral workings and henceforth teach only an exclusively Christian mysticism, to join him in working independently of the Order as a whole.

Shortly afterwards Waite and Blackden joined forces and set up their Temple, which, with little justification, retained the name of Isis-Urania. They appointed the Rev. W. A. Ayton, an elderly clergyman of strong alchemical interests, as their Third Chief. This latter figure was described by W. B. Yeats as one of the timidest men he had ever known; he urged Yeats never to participate in evocation as 'even the Olympic Planetary Spirits turn against us in the end'. His main interests were, as has been said, alchemical and he claimed to have once prepared the Elixir of Life although, alas, it evaporated before he had the opportunity to drink it![1] He was approaching ninety and must have been far too old to have played any real part in the government of the re-structured Isis-Urania. I have very little doubt that his functions therein were almost purely ornamental. After Ayton's death Waite and Blackden appointed

---

[1] The elixir was extremely volatile and a long-winded caller arrived just as the triumphant Alchemist had poured it out. When he returned to his laboratory the last drops were vapourising. I suspect this caller was the same man who caused Coleridge such distress; I have met him myself engaged in selling a magazine called the *Watchtower*.

Frater Non Sine Numine (Col. Webber) in his place.

The new Temple abandoned all magical work, abolished examinations within the Second Order and used heavily revised rituals designed to express a somewhat tortuous Christian mysticism. The ritual revisions had been carried out by Waite and it cannot be denied that the language used was exceedingly pompous and long-winded—or at least so it appears at the present day.

Meanwhile J. W. Brodie-Innes continued his Amen-Ra Temple in Edinburgh while Dr. Felkin and those London members who desired to carry on the magical tradition and the original Order scheme formed the Amoun Temple, changing the name of the Outer Order from Golden Dawn to Stella Matutina.[2]

[2] I suspect that, in the period 1900-1903 the Outer Order was known as the 'Mystic Rose'. Certainly the printed rules of *circa* 1902 refer to the Order as the 'Order of the M.R. in the Outer'.

Additional Note The late Israel Regardie's *Complete Golden Dawn System of Magic* (Falcon, 1984) includes two initiation rituals which are attributed to Waite's schismatic Golden Dawn. One of these is certainly authentic; the provenance of the other is something of a mystery.

Dr Woodman in full Masonic regalia

Dr Wynn Westcott robed as Supreme Magus of the 'Soc. Ros.'

Florence Farr as Rebecca West in Ibsen's *Rosmersholm*

W. B. Yeats

Aleister Crowley invoking Saturn (1910)

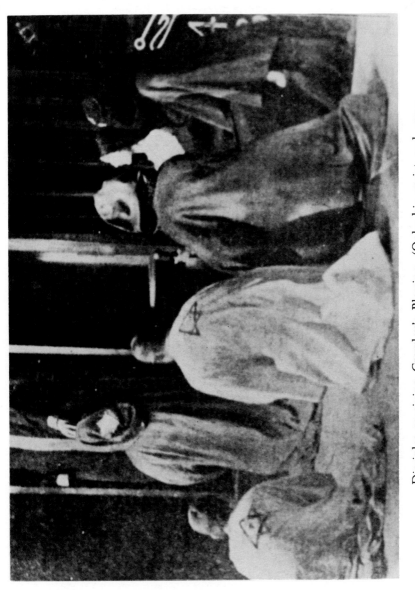

Disciples receiving Crowley's Blessing. (Only his waist and arms visible) 1910

Golden Dawn material found on a Sussex Beach in 1967

Members of a contemporary witch coven

CHAPTER ELEVEN

Dr. Felkin Seeks a Master

From the very commencement of the break with Mathers, Dr. Felkin was convinced that the Order must in some way manage to get back into communication with the Secret Chiefs. As early as May 3rd, 1902, he wrote:

> We beg to assure you that we are in entire sympathy with the view that if in fact the Order is without the guidance and inspiration of higher intelligences its rationale is gone. It occurred, however, to certain members that it might be possible, by reverting to the original constitution, to re-establish a link with the Third Order. There are now tangible grounds for believing that this step has not been taken in vain, and while we, as nominal chiefs, will not lightly yield allegiance to any force, power, or being purporting to act as the Third Order, the prospects seem to us sufficiently encouraging to warrant our own continued activity in the Order, and also we suggest your co-operation.

It is almost needless to say that the link referred to was an astral one and that the communications were received through trance mediumship and automatic writing of the type more or less familiarly found in modern spiritism. After the foundation of the Amoun Temple great importance was attached to these messages, now received in considerable number, and, while most of them were harmless enough in their effects, some of them gave approval to grave meddling with the Order's Rituals.

Even before the rebels had split into rival groups a tendency to tamper had existed and one of Annie Horniman's disagreements with Florence Farr arose from the latter's attempts to revise the Portal Ritual and withdraw the Portal lectures.[1]

Within the Stella Matutina this tendency was given full rein and we find, as has been stated, that this met with the approval of the Astral contacts, as is shown by the following communication regarding a revised Adeptus-Minor Ritual:

> The Inner and Secret Chiefs of the Third Order, unto the V.H. Frater F.R., Imperator of Amoun Temple, greeting.
>
> Hereby by the hand of Q.M. our scribe, we sanction and approve for general use the $5° = 6°$ ritual sent for approval, and which we herewith return. Delay in sanctioning this was unavoidable, as no word or letter or symbol of any ritual may be lawfully by the constitution of the Order be altered after once being sanctioned save by the consent of a Council of the Third Order, which only meets occasionally, or under powers conferred by them on certain Adepts. Yet shall ye not discard altogether the ritual previously in use, but shall retain the same and the copies thereof which ye have, for references and for use on special occasions if so ordered, but yet need make no new copies.
>
> The Password for the ensuing six months shall be Osiris Onophris—Osiris the Justified One, signifying that your zeal and the progress of your Temple have found favour with the Inner Chiefs of the Third Order, and that hereby ye are justified and signifying also that your hopes and trust must be in him whom the Lord of the Universe hath justified by whatsoever name men call him. Fare thee well.

Dr. Felkin was not satisfied with a merely astral meeting with the Third Order; he wanted physical contact and from the year 1901 onwards he travelled extensively on the continent in the hope of meeting authentic Rosicrucians—or so he

[1] Florence Farr and the other members of the 'Sphere' believed that the normal Golden Dawn qabalistic colour-scales (as given in Crowley's *777* and Torrens' *The Golden Dawn, its Inner Teachings*) were incorrect They had their own system of colour attributions and this has never been published.

told the Societas Rosicruciana in Anglia in a lecture he gave them on the subject of Rosicrucian Medicine.

In 1906 his efforts, so he believed, were crowned with success when he met:

> . . . a professor, his adopted daughter, and another gentleman near Hanover, who he believed were undoubtedly Rosicrucians. They were very secretive, and averse to giving much information, because they said that although they knew him as a scientific man, he was not a Mason, nor did he belong to any occult society that they had knowledge of. Owing to this, Frater F.R. immediately applied . . . and was initiated as a Freemason in Mary's Chapel, Edinburgh Lodge No. 1 on January 8th, 1907.[2]

It is interesting to note that the professor's adopted daughter claimed to be a niece of the original Anna Sprengel, Soror S.D.A., and said that her aunt had been a member of the same Rosicrucian organisation as herself.

The Rosicrucian group with which Felkin had made contact was led by Rudolf Steiner, the founder of the Anthroposophical Society, who was at that time still head of the German section of the Theosophical Society. Nevertheless, this group does not seem to have been Theosophical, either in an Adyar or Central European form, nor does it seem to have borne much resemblance to the later forms of Anthroposophy. Could it, one is inclined to incredulously wonder, have been the Ordo Templi Orientis,[3] of which Steiner was at that time the Austrian Chief? Certainly descriptions (from hostile sources admittedly) of Steiner's first Rosicrucian grade seem to show a marked resemblance between it and the first degree of the O.T.O. as as it was prior to its being re-written by Crowley.

Whatever the exact nature of Steiner's group it is certain that Felkin carried on a considerable correspondence with its chiefs and that in 1910 he sent a certain Mr. Meakin, Frater Ex Oriente Lux, to Germany as his personal representative.

[2] From Felkin's *History of the Amoun Temple*, written in 1912.
[3] Or some derivation thereof—but see Appendix E.

Before Meakin's departure he was consecrated as an Adeptus Minor. For some reason or other Felkin called in Waite to help perform this ceremony. It has been suggested to me that this was because Felkin and other members of the Amoun Temple were unsure whether they had true 'apostolic succession' from the original Golden Dawn. This suggestion seems to violate the principle of Occam's Razor; the simplest hypothesis is that Meakin wished to strengthen his position by representing as many Temples as possible. The previously quoted history of Amoun Temple then continues the narrative:

> These Fratres then said that in order to form a definite etheric link between themselves and Great Britain it was necessary for a Frater from Great Britain to be under their instruction for a year . . . Frater E.O.L. . . . commenced his teaching at once, and after residing for some time in North Germany and Austria, he was sent to Constantinople, and finally returned to Germany, where, having passed his tests, he was invited by special dispensation into the first few grades of the Rosicrucian Society, corresponding to our $6° = 5°$.

Both Dr. Felkin and his wife, known in the Order as Soror Quaestor Lucis, went to Germany in the summer of 1912. During their lengthy stay in that country they visited five different Temples and in these Temples they took part in ceremonies which, so Felkin said, conferred the grades of Adeptus Exemptus on his wife and Magister Templi on himself. He also seems to have had some form of medical treatment, devised by Steiner, during which coloured lights were played on him and healing ceremonies conducted in his presence. At the same time Felkin believed that some sort of concordat had been drawn up between himself and Steiner by which:

> Anyone conversant with German, French, Italian or Dutch, who is full $5° = 6°$, may be sent abroad with an introduction signed by F.R., and should it be considered that a candidate is sufficiently developed, one or more grades

may be given him. This is not essential, as, if the new methods are carefully introduced into our curriculum, the candidates will progress just as well without the necessity of going abroad.

The 'new' methods referred to were, of course, Steiner's system of physical and mental exercises.

Felkin's statements are so definite, and are borne out in such detail by Meakin, that it is curious to note that, in conversation with A. E. Waite in 1912, Steiner completely denied that he had conferred any grades whatsoever upon either Doctor or Mrs. Felkin. This does not necessarily invalidate Felkin's story, for Steiner may well have been suspicious of Waite—he knew that Waite led a rival Temple to Amoun—and decided, like Brer Rabbit, to lay low and say nuffin![4] In any case it seems unlikely that Steiner would have been so frank with Felkin and Meakin about his plans to create a vast occult international league if their relationship had been as distant as Waite believed.

The extent to which the leaders of the Stella Matutina were in Steiner's confidence is shown by the following extracts from a letter written by Meakin to the Danish[5] Baron Walleen, like himself a member of both the Stella Matutina and the German Order:

I have heard from Dr. Felkin of the proposed International Bund, which seems in many ways an excellent scheme to which I wish every success. As Dr. Steiner's name is so potent on the Continent, it is bound to prosper there. In England he has a band of admirers, but his name is not so generally known. The conditions in England are also peculiar. Dr. Steiner himself said to me that he recognised the difference. Therefore, I write to you, for we have a double tie—the Rosicrucian Fraternity of both the Continent and England;

---

[4] He was to repeat his denial some years later; but by this time Steiner was the head of a large international organisation and anxious to conceal his earlier ritualistic tendencies.

[5] For some reason the anonymous author of *Light Bearers of Darkness* gives his nationality as German and conceals his name.

we can speak freely. What I say now I wish to be laid before
Dr. Steiner by you, and the risk is mine. For if I do not speak
without fear or favour, no one else can.

Dr. Steiner is a statesman in his schemes. But a statesman,
when enquiring into the condition of a country unknown to
him, does not go only to the members of one party in it.
. . . In England the few members of the Continental Order are
all Theosophists, i.e. members of the T.S. They are none of
them members of the English Freemasons. They see things
from the T.S. point of view, and they have to use their
spectacles. I am the only member of the Continental Order
who is not and never has been a T.S. member;[6] I owe no
allegiance to Mrs. Besant. I am, as the Doctor knows, entirely
with him in the policy of abandoning Indian and Oriental
for European or Kabalistic training; I am also an English
Freemason, so that I can give him the point of view of the
other parties.

English occultism is roughly divided into (1) members of
the T.S., i.e. Mrs. Besant's followers headed by the co-Masons
in one sense; (2) members of the Hermetic Orders and Freemasons; (3) Independents, whether in small groups or
individuals.

The first class is the only one really known to the Doctor.
Of the second Dr. Felkin is very representative. Of the third
Mr. T.P. . . . Now when the Doctor comes to establish his
Bund there are certain considerations of great importance.
With regard to Group 1, the T.S. and its branches, I cannot
pretend to say what will happen. . . . The risk, however, is
with regard to groups 2 and 3. The Bund will, unless carefully managed, be regarded merely as a schism of the T.S. It
will command as much attention as the Quest Society of
G.R.S. Mead, and it may arouse great prejudice, for many
will take it exactly in the spirit in which England took the
German telegram to President Kruger. I am quite serious
when I say that to many the Bund will be thus considered—

---

[6] Dr. Felkin had formerly been a member of the Scottish Lodge of the
Theosophical Society.

'We don't care for Mrs. Besant any more than we cared for
Jameson and his raid, but after all Mrs. Besant is English;
who are these Germans to interfere?' It may sound ridiculous, but I know my country.

The next point, a very serious one indeed, is the attitude
of the Freemasons. This must be taken into consideration.
Here for a moment I must apparently digress. I wish to
contrast the working of groups 1, 2 and 3. Group 1 works
on the familiar lines of lectures, magazine publications, etc.
Dr. Steiner does much the same. Group 1 attracts a large
number of idle women who have the leisure to take a little
occultism with their afternoon tea, practically all the members are people with time and money. It attracts members,
but each lecturer is apt to get a personal following, hence
schisms, i.e. the Quest.

Group 2 is small in numbers. It works by Lodges and circu-
lates manuscripts. Its teaching is done by correspondence,
by individual officers etc. It seldom has lectures. It taps a
wholly different class, gets at more varied social strata, has
a far larger proportion of men. Being highly organised it has
more coherence; at the same time each Temple is apt to be
jealous of outside interferences. Most of its men are Freemasons. Some entire Temples are Freemasonic, e.g. the
Societas Rosicruciana in Anglia. Now these people are busy,
there are singularly few idle, moneyed or leisured woman
and men among them, they are very proud and independent.
In course of time, if they can get teaching in their own
manner, by MSS in circulation, by visits of members from
Lodge to Lodge, by or through their own Chiefs, I am
certain they will all, given time, join your Bund. But they
will not accept any T.S. dictation, they will not tolerate Chiefs
whom they do not know, they will not care for attending
cycles or lectures for which they have no time or inclina-
tion. These bodies are older than the T.S. and they do not
forget it. Humoured they will help you. If they are not
considered they will neither oppose you nor regard you.
They will simply leave the Bund alone exactly as they leave
the T.S. alone, the Co-Masons alone, etc. They must be got

at from within, not from without.

. . . Now I come to the Freemasonic point. Here I tread on very delicate ground. But I feel I must state the case, as I said without fear or favour. The Doctor is too great a man to be vexed with me. After all, all I wish to do is to secure that the best teaching reaches those most fit for it in the easiest way.

At present to establish a definite branch of the Continental Order giving grades, etc., in England will be a very difficult matter.[7] You are not yourself a Freemason. We sometimes call our Order, the Continental Order, Esoteric Masonry. The grades are closely akin to Freemasonry. Dr. Steiner indeed has some link with certain English or Scotch Masons—he gave me the name—from whom he derives a certain authority, a link in the physical.[8]

Now English Freemasonry is not occult, though it has occult lodges, and most English occultists not T.S. are Freemasons, if men. English Masonry boasts the Grand Lodge of 1717, the mother Lodge of the world. They are a proud, jealous autocratic body. Co-Masonry derives from the Grand Orient of France, an illegitimate body according to English ruling. No English Mason can work with Co-Masons.[9] Now the Masons who gave Dr. Steiner his link are regarded . . . as eccentrics who invent spurious grades. If the English Grand Lodge hears of anything called 'Esoteric Masonry', derived from such sources, under Chiefs once T.S. members, under a head in Berlin, it will not inquire who Dr. Steiner is or

[7] This sentence makes it quite clear that Steiner's 'International Bund' was not the ordinary Anthroposophical Society.

[8] The Masonic body alluded to was the Ancient and Primitive Rite of Memphis and Mizraim, centred in Manchester and led by John Yarker. Once again this links up with the O.T.O. whose chiefs were, without exception members of this Rite. It is interesting to note that Crowley eventually achieved the direction of this Rite some three years after he entered it in 1910.

[9] Yarker had recently established links between his clandestine, fee-snatching organisations and Annie Besant's Co-Masonry. He had admitted Wedgwood, the inventor of the ludicrous co-masonic 'Verulam working', into his Rite. Wedgwood later became a Bishop in the Liberal Catholic Church, but eventually had to be prevented from preaching; his habit of stripping naked in the pulpit was too much for his congregation!

what is the nature of his work; it will simply say 'no English Masons of the Free and Accepted Masons may join any society working pseudo-Masonic Rites, i.e. no one of ordinary accepted Freemasonry can attend any meetings or take any grades in this illegitimate body! Finis!

Then we who are members of Dr. Steiner's Lodge and are Freemasons will be in a sad plight. At present this would affect only myself and, well, Dr. Felkin too. But if Esoteric Masonry is breathed of in England, and the fiat goes against it, no English Mason will wish to join the Bund.

After all this cold water, you will ask what useful suggestion do I imagine I have to make. Well, perhaps nothing very useful. Still this is my practical suggestion. Let the Bund be started. Let Messrs. S. and C. get all the MSS they can, and let them establish relations with the bodies in Group 2. Either let them supply such written teaching as can be given to the heads of the Lodges that will come in, and seek no interference with the Lodges, or let them form a definite committee under Dr. Steiner with representative people on it. All this must be done slowly.

The system of having people in the Lodges like Dr. Felkin to teach 'processes' within Group 2 is the most practical, and to join an English Lodge, to go between England and the Continent, and to get the written teaching will probably work well enough.

But if a Lodge of the Continental Order is to be established in England, Dr. Steiner will be faced with the Masonic difficulty. This is really serious, and no one of the T.S. will understand it, nor even any Continental Freemasons. Look at my position and again at Dr. Felkin's—either we were banned from all association with Freemasons, i.e. from practically all Lodges in Group 2, or else from association with the Bund. Either we must be cut off again, or our usefulness for general purposes is gone. If Dr. Steiner would summon one or two non-Theosophical persons to discuss with him, he would see this at once. The practical solution will be found in a compromise. If he avoids the name 'Esoteric Masonry' and allows perhaps a ritual like those used in the Societas Rosicruciana or in the S(tella) M(atutina), and has for officers in England a mixed group, including the Heads of the chief Hermetic Lodges, etc. . . . as well as T.S. people and a few who will join anything of Dr. Steiner's— it will succeed. Otherwise I fear that only a few T.S. people and a few whom Dr. Felkin and myself . . . can influence directly, will be all that will join at the outset. As a Theosophist Schism, and a foreign intrusive Masonic Schism, the Bund will arouse every possible English prejudice against it. Devoted to the Doctor as we are, we should both regret it.

This letter seems to have had a marked effect upon Steiner's plans, for when he came to establish a formal organisation in England after the first World War there were no secret ritual initiations, no Esoteric Masonry, but instead an open society organisationally similar to the Theosophical Society.

On the basis of the observations he had made in Germany Dr. Felkin constructed new Stella Matutina grades of Adeptus Major, Adeptus Exemptus and Magister Templi. I have examined these grades in manuscript and, apart from elaborations clearly introduced by Felkin,[10] there is a certain likeness between them and the IV, V, and VI grades of the Ordo Templi Orientis before they were re-written by Aleister Crowley.

After their alleged German initiations Dr. Felkin and his wife temporarily departed for New Zealand. Here they set up a new Stella Matutina Temple called Smaragdine Thalasses and closely associated with the New Zealand Province of the Societas Rosicruciana. At first they had intended their stay in New Zealand to be a permanent one, but Meakin, who was to have taken over the Chiefship of the Amoun Temple, had died in the Autumn of 1912,[11] so after a comparatively short time they returned to England in order to train successors. This was done, but in such haste and with such a lack of discrimi-

---

[10] In constructing these rituals Felkin padded out what he had seen in Germany with extracts from Mabel Collins' neglected inspirational work *Light on the Path* and the Egyptian *Papyrus of Ani*.

[11] The 'astral masters' of the Stella Matutina were most surprised by this death; 'he just slipped out' they said.

nation that great trouble was later to result therefrom.

The Felkins took up permanent residence in New Zealand in 1916, but, before they finally departed from England, Dr. Felkin took it upon himself to set up three new Temples and promulgate a new constitution by which he retained the Chieftainship of the Stella Matutina although he was no longer Imperator of the Mother Temple. In spite of the outbreak of war he still retained a strong desire to work with Steiner's followers, as is shown by the following extract from his statement of June 18th, 1916:

As you are aware, I can personally permit any branch Rosicrucian Societies to be started. . . . I propose, before leaving England, to form three such branches. . . . The two I propose to form in London could either pay you a yearly sum for the use of the Temple and Vault, on a definite day to be settled by you. . . . With regard to a Branch in Bristol,[12] which I am going to form, they can at present work their Outer entirely there, and make arrangements with you when they have any candidates for the Inner.

. . . The first London Daughter Temple will be confined to the members of the Societas Rosicruciana in Anglia, who have taken at least Grade 4. I may mention here that the reason why I am obliged to form it is as follows: When E.O.L. and I made our arrangements for recognition by our Continental Fratres, they stipulated, and he agreed, that the Masonic Rosicrucians, of whom there are large numbers, should be given the opportunity of being linked with us.

With regard to the third daughter Temple, there are some fifty or sixty members of the Temple which used to be ruled by S.R.[13] and a number of the members of the Anthroposophical Society who are seeking admission. It has been pointed out to me, that as these people have worked on different lines from us, it would not be well to admit them to

[12] The Bristol Temple was called Hermes, it later became almost exlusively Anthroposophical but it has a certain importance, as we shall see in a later chapter, as one of the ancestors of an authentic Golden Dawn Temple still operating at the present day.
[13] S.R.—Sacramentum Regis, i.e. A. E. Waite.

the S.M., as they would undoubtedly cause confusion in the S.M. Temple. I therefore propose that they should form a Temple of their own. . . .

. . . I take full responsibility for the formation of these three Daughter Temples, and it rests with you to do all in your power to help them to be an added power to the Rosicrucian Movement.

Our password for the present six months is ACHAD, signifying 'Unity', and it is my great desire that all the scattered Rosicrucian Forces without our reach should be gathered together into a harmonious whole. . . .

In this last-expressed hope Dr. Felkin was, as we shall see in a later chapter, doomed to disappointment.

CHAPTER TWELVE

. . . . . . And Brodie-Innes
Finds One

From the very moment that it became clear to Mathers that
any reconciliation with the rebels was impossible for, at the
very least, a considerable period of time, he made hectic efforts
to re-establish a foothold in London—for while the Bradford
and Weston-super-Mare Temples seem to have remained loyal
to him, their numbers were so few as to be insignificant. At
first his hopes were centred on Crowley, but these were blighted
by a violent quarrel resulting from the latter's extended stay
in the Far East, temporary conversion to orthodox Hinyana
Buddhism, and attempts to get Mathers to take up the same
religious position. After this quarrel all Crowley's previous
admiration for his Chief seems to have turned to hatred; in
May 1904 we find him writing in his notebook '. . . a special
task find a man who can go to entrap Mathers. Let him
read Levi; then go.' In the following summer he evoked Beelzebub to consecrate talismans designed to be used against the
Golden Dawn,[1] and in the same year he claimed that Mathers
was obsessed by Abramelin demons and that Mr. and Mrs.
Mathers were under the control of Madame Horos and her
husband.

[1] To be quite fair to Crowley it should be stated that he looked upon
these activities as being merely self-defence; for he believed, probably quite
rightly, that Mathers was trying to use Black Magic against him. When
Crowley's bloodhounds suddenly died he attributed their sudden demise
to the activities of Mathers.

The investigation of a competent Skryer into the house of
of our unhappy Fra., confirmed this divination; neither our
Fra., nor his Hermetic Mul., were there seen; but only the
terrible shapes of the evil Adepts S.V.A.[2] and H., whose
original bodies having been sequestered by Justice, were no
longer of use to them.

MacGregor Mathers then proceeded to appoint Dr. Berridge
at his London representative and the latter was soon working
the ceremonies and rites of the Golden Dawn in a new Temple
situated in West London. In his autobiography, *Shadows of
Life and Thought*, A. E. Waite states that he was approached
by members of this Temple who alleged that it was grossly
mismanaged and that the ceremonial vestments used in Temple
were in a verminous condition; he goes on to say that this
Temple subsequently 'flickered out'. If this was so it is certain
that the 'flickering' extended over a considerable period, for
Berridge's Temple was operative as early as 1903 and I possess
the notebooks and letters of an Adeptus Minor, dated *circa*
1913, the contents of which show that there were twenty-
three members of a flourishing Second Order under the Berridge-
Mathers obedience at that date.

Meanwhile J. W. Brodie-Innes continued the direction of
the Amen-Ra Temple, slowly coming to the conclusion that
the revolt had, from the very beginning, been unjustified. He
made tentative, conciliatory approaches to Mathers and finally
came to accept him as the rightful Chief of the Order and the
only genuine representative of the Masters. By 1908, when
Mathers returned, at least temporarily, to England[3] he and
Brodie-Innes were in complete accord and in 1913 we find
Brodie-Innes writing to Felkin:

> . . . I have stacks of MSS and teachings going to far further

[2] S.V.A.=Swami Viva Ananda—this, it will be remembered, was one of
the aliases of Madame Horos.

[3] I suspect, but cannot prove, that Mathers subsequently returned permanently to Paris. Certainly he made frequent visits there, for he was
initiating Americans in the Ahathoor Temple right up to the outbreak of
the war in 1914.

lengths than I used to think possible. . . .[4] I received the MSS as deputy Archon Basileus in this country. My commission as such comes from the Third Order—or not to make any ambiguity of these words from those Higher Adepts whom I so term—and I can pass them on to such as acknowledge my authority and position. This of course also involves recognition of Mathers who has committed his authority to me.

Brodie-Innes had found the Master he sought. Never again was there to be any doubt of his loyalty, and when Mathers died he wrote a moving and affectionate obituary which was published in the *Occult Review*, where it did something to counter the astonishing bad taste of A. E. Waite's sneering comments published in a previous issue.

At about the time of the conclusion of this alliance between the two occultists the name of the Outer Order was changed from Golden Dawn to Alpha et Omega—usually abbreviated to A.O.—and Brodie-Innes assumed a general charge over the English and Scottish Temples while Mathers concentrated on building up his Ahathoor Temple and extending his American connection.

According to Regardie the Golden Dawn had spread to the U.S.A. before 1900 and a Thoth-Hermes Temple had been established in Chicago. Certainly, many Americans received Parisian initiations during the period 1907-1914, and it is alleged by more than one source that in return for high fees Mathers admitted people to supposedly high grades far beyond the actual attainments of the people concerned; in his 'Equinox' Crowley sneered at a woman who, he said, had paid hundreds of dollars for the nominal grade of Exempt Adept. By the commencement of the First World War Mathers had succeeded in not only establishing two or three American Temples, but in bringing the Masonic Societas Rosicruciana in America increasingly under the influence of himself and his followers.

Throughout this pre-war period A. E. Waite carried on his Isis-Urania Temple, at first in a somewhat shaky peaceful co-

[4] See Appendix D for some details of these further teachings.

existence with the Amoun Temple of the Stella Matutina and then, when Waite brought the concordat to an end, (probably because he disapproved of Dr. Felkin's attempting to establish a more friendly relationship with Brodie-Innes) in complete independence.

Waite states that he brought his Temple to an end in 1914[5] owing to 'internecine feuds over documents'. This is probably a reference to the fact that a majority of the Adepti had a strong objection to Waite's attempt to institute new rituals written by himself in place of the already heavily amended Golden Dawn ceremonies. These new rituals were privately printed (*circa* 1915) in ten small red-bound books;[6] although they are based on a symbolic ascent of the Tree of Life they bear little resemblance to the G.D. system. A few initiates seem to have joined Waite in working the new scheme but, as we have seen in the previous chapter, the majority entered a new Stella Matutina Temple under Felkin.

Perhaps the major achievement of Waite's Temple was to number amongst its members Evelyn Underhill and Charles Williams. While the first named seems to have found Waite lacking in those things for which she was looking—although I suspect that she owes a little more to Waite and a little less to Von Hugel than is generally recognised—Charles Williams' whole outlook and philosophy were permanently affected by Waite's version of the Golden Dawn.

I have completed a lengthy analysis of the influence of the Golden Dawn and the Christian Qabalah on the poetry and prose of Charles Williams; suffice it for the moment to say that the Golden Dawn system—or to be more correct Waite's heterodox version of that system—is the key without which the deepest and inmost meaningfulness of Williams can never be unlocked.

[5] I suspect that this date should be 1915 or 1916—other dates are quite definitely wrong given by Waite.

[6] I have seen an earlier version dated 1910. These are not so heavily amended and bear more resemblance to the scheme outlined in the cipher manuscripts and first elaborated by Mathers.

CHAPTER THIRTEEN

The Astrum Argentinum and the O.T.O.

In Cairo, on three days in April 1904, Aleister Crowley (Frater Perdurabo) received a direct-voice communication from an allegedly non-human entity called Aiwass. This communication was entitled Liber AL vel Legis, the Book of the Law, and it was this extraordinary prose-poem, of only three short chapters, that made Crowley decide to not only establish a new religion designed to replace Christianity, but to build a new Rosicrucian Order with himself as its Chief. He first announced his assumption of the Headship of the Order in his edition of the 'Goetia', referring to himself as 'our Illustrious and ever-Glorious Frater, ye wise Perdurabo, that Myghte Chiefe of ye Rosy-Cross Fraternitye.' Around this time he drew up, in skeletonic form, revised Golden Dawn rituals in which the characters of the Stele of Revealing and Liber AL—Nuit, Hadit, Ra-Hoor-Khuit, Bes-na-Maut, Tanech and Ankh-f-n-Khonsu—take up the visible and invisible stations of the Officers in the Temple. The rough notes following are an example of the ideas he had in mind:

> This is the ritual of the passing through the waters; but the Invocations are to be got from the Egyptian papyri as taught. . . .
> There are thirteen parts; the Key is the Hanged Man of the Tarot for water is the thirteenth letter.
> 1. Without a word of warning the candidate is taken to

the Chamber of Initiation and affixed to a great cross in a position to cause some pain. There is no support for the head. He is left alone.

2. In silence Hoor-pa-kraat is invoked—as in old ritual—to defend him.

3. He is taken down and tried as in the *Book of the Dead.* Being found guilty.

4. He is stripped of all attributes—banishing all symbols —and made naked, after which he is

5. Scourged.

6. It being now mid-day, the adoration is made to the exalted Ahathoor.

7. He is left as dead.

8. It being now midnight, the adoration is made unto Khephra the Beetle.

9. The Ankh is made upon him, and he is raised to life, and clothed in the robe of rose and gold.

10. The wand of D.P. is given to him.

11. He is given the sword.

12. The insight of Horus is given unto him in the power of Hoor and Isis. He is Asar.

13. The magical force is roused in him; he hath ecstasy. In that ecstasy he is left to do what he will.

The officers are always Ankh-f-na-Khonsu, Bes-n-Maut, Tanech—For open work he can wear the Abramelin things with the Ankh-f-na-Khonsu symbol.

By the time Crowley eventually founded his Order (1907) he seems to have abandoned these plans. Instead he decided to use only slightly amended versions of the Golden Dawn rituals. The grade-structure was left intact but with the names of the grades altered as follows:

G.D. Grade	A.A.[1] Grade
Neophyte	Probationer
Zelator	Neophyte
Theoricus	Zelator

[1] Astrum Argentinum—Silver Star—was the name of Crowley's Order, not 'Atlantean Adepts' as stated in several printed sources.

114

G.D. Grade	A.A. Grade
Practicus	Practicus
Philosophus	Philosophus
Lord of the Paths of the Portal	Dominus Liminus
Adeptus Minor	Adeptus Minor

The magical teachings and practises used in the A.A. during its early period were those of the Golden Dawn (although Crowley completely rewrote the MSS, often in a much more easily comprehensible form), with a certain amount of Yoga and other oriental practices grafted on to them.

Crowley soon began (March 1909) to publish his magazine *The Equinox* as the official organ of the A.A., and this he continued to do for the next five years. In the second number of this periodical the rituals of the Outer Order were published in an abbreviated form—in accordance, so Crowley later said, with the instructions of the Secret Chiefs—and it was announced that the rituals of the R.R. et A.C. would be published in the next issue. Mathers, much alarmed, obtained a temporary injunction restraining Crowley from publication but, as he was in considerable financial difficulty at the time, was unable to afford to set into motion the legal machinery required to obtain a perpetual injunction. Later Mathers was granted a second temporary injunction, but on appeal this was set aside, on the grounds of Mathers' failure to proceed with the main action, and Crowley proceeded to publish.

All this gave a certain amount of publicity to the A.A., but it was not until later in the same year that Crowley's celebration of the Rites of Eleusis at Caxton Hall brought the Order into real prominence in the public eye.

The Rites of Eleusis were a series of seven invocations of the gods and were constructed upon the basis of Leila Waddel's violin playing, Victor Neuburg's dancing, and the poetry of Crowley—the latter supplemented by a little Swinburne. The fee of five guineas for the series was a considerable amount at the time, and, making allowance for this, they were surprisingly successful.

The reviews were on the whole favourable—the *Sketch* in particular—but the rites were strongly attacked by the *Looking*

Glass, a newly-established magazine specialising in scandal-mongering and share pushing:

After depositing our hat and coat with an attendant we were conducted by our guide to a door, at which stood a rather dirty looking person attired in a sort of imitation Eastern robe, with a drawn sword in his hand, who, after inspecting our cards, admitted us to a dimly lighted room heavy with incense. Across this room low stools were placed in rows, and when we arrived a good many of these were already occupied by various men and women, for the most part in evening dress.

At the extreme end of the room was a heavy curtain, and in front of this sat a huddled-up figure in draperies, beating a kind of monotonous tom-tom.

When we had all been admitted the doors were shut, and the light, which had always been exceedingly dim, was completely extinguished except for a slight flicker on the 'altar'. Then after a while more ghostly figures appeared on the stage, and a person in a red hood, supported on each side by a blue-chinned gentleman in a sort of Turkish bath costume, commenced to read some gibberish to which the attendants made response at intervals.

Our guide informed us that this was known as the banishing rite of the pentagram.

More Turkish bath attendants then appeared, and executed a kind of Morris dance around the stage. Then the gentleman in the red cloak, supported by brothers Aquarius and Capricornus—the aforesaid blue-chinned gentleman—made fervent appeals to the Mother of Heaven to hear them, and after a little while a not unprepossessing lady appeared, informed them that she was the Mother of Heaven, and asked if she could do anything for them. . . . They beg her to summon the Master, as they wish to learn from him if there is any God, or if they are free to behave as they please. The Mother of Heaven thereupon takes up a violin and plays not unskilfully for about ten minutes, during which time the room is again plunged in complete darkness. The playing is succeeded by a loud hammering, in which all the robed figures on the stage join, and after a din sufficient to wake the Seven Sleepers the lights are turned up a little and a figure appears from a recess and asks what they want. They beseech him to let them know if there is really a God, as, if not, they will amuse themselves without any fear of the consequences. 'The Master' promises to give the matter his best attention, and, after producing a flame from the floor by the simple expedient of lifting a trap-door, he retires with the Mother of Heaven for 'meditation', during which time darkness again supervenes. After a considerable period he returns, flings aside a curtain on the stage, and declares that the space behind it is empty, and that there is no God. He then exhorts his followers to do as they like and make the most of this life.

The same article went on to imply that some sexual irregularities were taking place in the semi-darkness—great play was made of a perfectly ordinary photograph of Leila Waddel kneeling on Crowley's chest—and to promise further revelations in the future. Two further attacks followed—much of the information seems to have been supplied by Mathers—and there were some resignations from the A.A. Crowley refused to sue, although he wrote a spirited defence of the Rites of Eleusis for for the *Bystander*, but G. C. Jones, who considered a passing reference to himself as slanderous, issued a writ for defamation. This action was tried in April 1911 (I have already mentioned the cross-examination of Mathers), a great deal of mud was thrown, much of which proved to be sticky, and Jones lost his case.

This did considerable damage to Crowley's Order, for not only did he lose some of his most able members (the departure of J. F. C. Fuller must have been a particularly severe blow), but the supply of new entrants diminished almost to vanishing point; few were anxious to be members of any Order led by a man of Crowley's reputation.

Contrary to popular belief sexual magic and the techniques of left-handed Tantricism played no part whatsoever in the

Astrum Argentinum as such—although, of course, individual members of the Order may have used these methods. It is true, of course, that long before 1907 Crowley had come to the conclusion that an active sexual life was no bar to magical success—he had his own interpretation of the chastity traditionally demanded of the advanced occultist—but, apart from one or two exceptional incidents, I do not believe he practiced sexual magic until 1912, at which time he came into contact with modern German Templarism.

In the fourteenth century the original Knights Templar had been suppressed throughout Europe; nominally on the grounds of heresy, sodomy and bestiality, but more probably because their vast wealth had excited the avarice of the feudal rulers of Christendom. Only in Portugal, where there were no doubts of the Knights' orthodoxy, did the Templars survive as the Order of Christ.

It was not until some four hundred years later that European occultists began to take any considerable interest in the Order of the Temple, but by the middle of the eighteenth century numerous freemasons attached to the continental highgrades had come to the conclusion that the building activities of the Templars and the fact that the symbolism of the masonic craft-degrees centred round the building of Solomon's Temple established some historical link between the two Orders.

Within a short time there were numerous fraternities claiming a Templar origin; in Europe there was the Stricte Observance, in Scotland the Royal Order, and in England there were many Templar encampments. Later still, in France, arose the Order of the Temple, using an unorthodox version of the Gospel of St. John and relying on an eighteenth-century forgery, the so-called Charter of Larmenius, to prove its bona fides.

The *Ordo Templi Orientis*, founded at the beginning of the twentieth century by a German high-grade freemason and occultist named Karl Kellner, was thus only the last of a long line of allegedly Templar organisations, and, like its predecessors, its origins are a little mysterious.

Kellner had originally wanted to start the O.T.O. in the middle of the 'nineties, but those he wished to have as his co-workers were, at the time, heavily involved in an unsuccessful attempt to revive the eighteenth-century Order of the Illuminati.

In 1902 John Yarker, the Manchester-based head of various masonic and pseudo-masonic rites, chartered three German occultists, named Reuss, Hartmann, and Klein, to establish a German Grand Lodge of the 'Ancient and Primitive Rite of Memphis and Mizraim'[2] and the 'Ancient and Accepted Scottish Rite of Cerneau'. This they duly did and they also started a magazine called the *Oriflamme*, the early issues of which, so I believe, contain no mention of the O.T.O., although they do, of course, mention 'Memphis and Mizraim'.

As early as 1904, however, the magazine mentioned the O.T.O., headed by Kellner, and referred to a 'great secret' of which this Order had custody. In 1912 a jubilee edition of the *Oriflamme* revealed this secret with almost brutal frankness:

Our Order possesses the KEY which opens up all Masonic and Hermetic secrets, namely, the teaching of sexual magic, and this teaching explains, without exception, all the secrets of Nature, all the symbolism of Freemasonry and all systems of religion.

In other words, the Order taught a type of sexual illuminism similar to, if not identical with, the left-hand Path[3] of Bengali Tantricism.

---

[2] It is not my intention to waste a great amount of space on the involved history of spurious and clandestine masonic organisations but it should perhaps be explained that both the Rite of Memphis, organised in no less than ninety degrees, and the Rite of Mizraim, organised in ninety-seven degrees, were of early nineteenth century origin. The rites had fallen into the hands of Yarker who, in 1875, had unified them and heavily revised their rituals. The 'Ancient and Accepted Scottish Rite of Cerneau' was Yarker's spurious rival to the genuine 'Ancient and Accepted Rite' which still flourishes today.

[3] Contrary to popular belief the term 'left-hand' has no moral significance in the terminology of Tantricism. It merely expresses the fact that in Tantric rites culminating in physical sexual intercourse the female devotee who represents the Goddess sits on the left-hand side of the operator while in those ceremonies in which union is merely symbolic the woman sits on the practitioner's right-hand side.

Kellner claimed to have derived his methods from three oriental adepts, one Arab and two Hindu, but a more immediate source seems to have been a group of European followers of the American occultist P. B. Randolph. Randolph suffered from an acute persecution complex—possibly not unreasonably in view of his partial negro ancestry—and took care to conceal his unusual sexual doctrines beneath a cloak of heavily-veiling symbolism; even close associates seem to have had no inkling of them, and it is significant that R. Swinburne Clymer, who later became chief of the organisations founded by Randolph, regarded any form of sexual magic as the blackest of black magic. Nevertheless, Randolph did pass on his teachings to a trusted and tiny group of his French followers who subsequently called themselves the Hermetic Brotherhood of the Light, a name used by more than one group of nineteenth-century occultist. It was possibly from one or more members of this group that Kellner derived the techniques used in the O.T.O. although, of course, he certainly met Tantrics in the course of his oriental wanderings. It is interesting to note that a group ultimately deriving from Randolph has survived in France to this day and that the sexual teachings are identical with those of the O.T.O.

The Ordo Templi Orientis was organised in nine operative grades with a tenth purely administrative grade.[4] The grades up to and including the sixth were ritually conferred and were largely concerned with the Order's unorthodox interpretation of Masonic symbolism. The seventh, eighth, and ninth grades were concerned with sexual magic; there were no rituals for these grades, the new members were simply handed written material giving the grade instructions. The lectures for the eighth grade taught a particular type of autosexual activity— a sort of magical masturbation—which, to the best of my knowledge, has no oriental analogue, while that for the ninth grade was concerned with heterosexual magic.

The formula of the ninth degree was given by Crowley, under

---

[4] There were also various sub-grades. Later Aleister Crowley evolved an eleventh grade; this was concerned with homosexual magic similar to that found in certain heterodox Sufi sects.

the veil of symbolism, in various of his publicly printed English writings and more explicitly in his *De Nuptiis Secretis Deorum cum Hominibus* and his *De Homunculus*; these latter works have not been published in their original English but German translations were printed before the first World War. Curiously enough, however, the clearest and most detailed printed account of this process is given in the penultimate chapter of Israel Regardie's *Tree of Life* where it is presented under the conventional terminology of alchemy :

> Through the stimulus of warmth and spiritual fire to the Athanor there should be a transfer, an ascent of the Serpent from that instrument into the Cucurbite, used as a retort. The alchemical ma..iage or the mingling of the two streams of force in the retort causes at once the chemical corruption of the Serpent in the menstruum of the Gluten, this being the Solve part of the general alchemical formula of Solve et Coagula. Hard upon the corruption of the Serpent and his death, arises the resplendent Phoenix which, as a talisman, should be charged by means of a continuous invocation of the spiritual principle conforming to the work in hand. The conclusion of the Mass consists in either the consumption of the transubstantiated elements, which is the Amrita, or the anointing and consecration of a special talisman.

This is followed by an unattributed quotation which Regardie claims is an alchemical description of the so-called 'Mass of the Holy Ghost'; in fact it is a quotation from the 'Azoth' of M. Georgius Beatus and it seems impossible to give the passage any sexual interpretation when it is read in its context.[5]
Regardie goes on:

> By some authorities it is roughly estimated that from the preliminary invocation, with the binding of the forces in the elements, to the act of taking the Communion itself from

---

[5] Whether any Western alchemical texts can legitimately be given a sexual interpretation is a moot point. On the other hand there seems little

the consecrated Chalice, the operation should not take less than an hour. Sometimes, indeed, a much longer period is required, especially if it is required that the charging of the talisman be complete and thorough. Great care is required to prevent the unguarded loss of the elements. There is the possibility of actual leakage or an overflowing from the Cucurbite and the assimilation or evaporation of the corrupted elements within that instrument is also an accident greatly to be deplored. It cannot be stressed too strongly or too frequently that if the elements are not consecrated aright, or in the first place if the invoked force does not properly impinge upon or is insecurely bound within the elements, the whole operation may be nullified. And it may easily degenerate to the lowest depths, resulting in the creation of a Qlipothic horror to exist like a vampire upon the un-naturally sensitive and those who are inclined to hysteria and obsession. If the elixir be properly distilled, serving as the medium of the invoked spirit, then the Heavens are opened, and the Gates swing back for the Theurgist, and the treasures of the earth are laid at his feet.

Crowley entered the IX° of the O.T.O.[6] in 1912 at the personal invitation of Theodor Reuss (who had become Outer Head of the Order on the death of Kellner in 1905) and travelled to Berlin for his initiation and appointment as 'Supreme and Holy King of Ireland, Iona and all the Britains within the Sanctuary of the Gnosis'—Crowley's official title as Chief of a British subsidiary Order entitled the Mysteria Mystica Maxima. It is clear that at first Crowley regarded his new organisation

doubt that almost all Chinese Taoist alchemy was concerned with a type of sexual magic; the 'cinnabar' (mercury) and 'sulphur' from which the Elixir of Life were to be manufactured were the male and female sexual secretions. *The Secret of the Golden Flower* was concerned with this type of alchemy; the translation of the work with an introduction by Jung is only a small part of the whole. Neither Jung, Wilhelm, or the latter's Chinese colleague had access to the whole work, nor did any of them know anything of sexual magic, hence all of them misunderstood the nature of the *Golden Flower*. Allen and Unwin will shortly be publishing a book which quite definitely establishes the sexual nature of Chinese alchemy.

[6] Crowley had probably been a member of the VI° of the O.T.O. since 1910, when Reuss first came to see him.

as merely (*a*) a useful preliminary to membership of the Astrum Argentinum and (*b*) a splendid way of exacting sizeable initiation fees from the credulous.

The 'Manifesto of the M.M.M.', issued in 1912, reads as though considerable parts of it had been written by a professional salesman of gold bricks; the 'privileges' of members of the Order are described as follows:

1. They have not only access to, but instruction in, the whole body of hidden knowledge preserved in the Sanctuary from the beginning of its manifestation. In the lower grades the final secrets are hinted, and conveyed in symbol, beneath veil, and through sacrament. In this way the intelligence of the initiate is called into play, so that he who well uses the knowledge of the lower grades may be selected for invitation to the higher, where all things are declared openly.

2. They become partakers of the current of Universal Life in Liberty, Beauty, Harmony, and Love which flames within the heart of the O.T.O., and the Light of that august fraternity insensibly illuminates them ever more and more as they approach its central Sun.

3. They meet those persons most complemental to their own natures, and find unexpected help and brotherhood in the whole world wherever they may travel.

4. They obtain the right to sojourn in the secret houses of the O.T.O., permanently or for a greater or lesser period of the year according to their rank in the Order; or in the case of those of the Fifth and lower degrees, are candidates for invitation to these houses.

5. The Knowledge of the Preparation and Use of the Universal Medicine is restricted to members of the IX°; but it may be administered to members of the VIII° and VII° in special circumstances by favour of the National Grand Masters General, and even in particular emergency to members of lower degrees.

6. In the V° all members are pledged to bring immediate and perfect relief to all distress of mind, body, or estate, in which they may find any of their fellows of that degree. In higher

degrees the Bonds of Fraternity are still further strengthened. The Order thus affords a perfect system of insurance against every misfortune or accident of life.

7. Members of the IX° become part proprietors of the Estates and Goods of the Order, so that the attainment of this degree implies a return with interest of the fees and subscriptions paid.

8. The Order gives practical assistance in life to worthy members of even its lower degrees, so that, even if originally poor, they become well able to afford the comparatively high fees of the VII°, VIII° and IX°. On exaltation to the IV° each Companion may file an account of his circumstances, and state in what direction he requires help.

The Manifesto was illustrated with flattering photographs of Boleskine House 'in order that those intending to apply to the Grand Secretary General for admission to the Order may understand that its purely material advantages are sufficient compensation for the fees demanded, and that the Gift of God is indeed without money and without price.'[7]

The fees charged to initiates of the M.M.M. were large; a member of the IX° would have paid a total of £103.10.0d. in initiation fees—a very considerable sum at the time—and, in addition, an annual subscription of £34.13.0d.

From 1912 until 1914 Crowley made only desultory experiments in the practice of sexual magic; in the latter year, however, he obtained considerable success in his 'Paris Working'—an invocation of Jupiter and Mercury—by using sexual techniques and from then onwards he concentrated almost exclusively on his ninth degree workings and experiments. The results of these, over a period of about four years, were recorded in the three (unpublished) volumes of *Rex De Arte Magica*.[8]

[7] Officially authorship of this manifesto was attributed to 'L. Bathurst IX° Grand Secretary General' (L. Bathurst was, in fact, Crowley's mistress, the Australian violinist Leila Waddell) but the style is clearly Crowley's and he must have revised her work.

[8] There are three surviving typescripts of the first and third volumes. The second volume survives in a copy in the ownership of a Swedish private collector who, while he gave me the sight of a few pages of it, felt unable to allow me to either read the entire volume or to make photostats of any part of it.

The A.A. ceased all group work in London when Crowley left for America in late 1914; after this Crowley's London disciples seem to have confined their Lodge activities to working the first six grades of the O.T.O. under the guidance of Crowley's London representative, a well-known, highly moral, and unquestionably sincere spiritualist medium.

This activity ceased in 1916 when the Metropolitan Police raided the O.T.O.'s London quarters at 93 Regent Street and removed a quantity of Temple furniture, masonic regalia, etc., 'for examination'; this material was never returned. While the raid was supposedly organised merely to investigate allegedly fraudulent mediumistic practices it was, in reality, a reprisal for Crowley's pro-German activities in the U.S.A. An abortive effort to resume Lodge-work in London was made in the 'twenties by some of Crowley's English disciples but their tentative scheme was abandoned under the threat of extremely hostile newspaper publicity.[9] From then onwards Crowley normally initiated English-speaking candidates for O.T.O. membership by giving them drafts of the rituals and then getting them to build up the Temple and go through the rituals astrally in much the same way as initiates of the Golden Dawn travelled up the Tree of Life in the course of their astral 'Path-workings'.

According to Crowley's own account he became head of the O.T.O. in 1922, Theodor Reuss having resigned in his favour, and it is certainly true that for a brief period in 1924/25 he was recognised as such by a majority of the members of the Order. After the Book of the Law had been translated into German, however, the overwhelming majority of the German initiates were so shocked by the book's third chapter that they withdrew this recognition and continued an O.T.O. quite independently of Crowley under the leadership of a certain Frater Recnartus. From then on there were two organisations calling themselves the O.T.O., the first largely German-speaking and re-

[9] I have in my possession a magical work presented by 'Baphomet XI°30°33°97°' (Crowley) to 'Benjamin Charles Hammond VII°30°33°95°' and in a series of notes on the flyleaf Hammond tells in some detail of the persecutions and pressures inflicted on him and his fellow-Thelemites in the process of dissuading them from opening an active O.T.O. Temple.

garding Crowley as a black-magician, the second largely English-speaking, but including at least one German lodge, and having Crowley as its Chief.

The active Temple-work of both organisations ceased in Germany in 1937, when, together with other occult bodies, they were suppressed by the Nazis.

CHAPTER FOURTEEN

Dr. Felkin's Astral Junkies

It will be remembered that, on his final departure to New
Zealand, Dr. Felkin had expressed the wish that there should
be 'unity among the scattered Rosicrucian forces'. What, in
fact, happened, was that the Chiefs of the Amoun Temple in
London became as addicted to mediumship and astral travel as
a drug-addict is to heroin! They buried themselves in the
seething images of their own unconscious minds to such good
effect that two of them became schizophrenic—one of them,
a clergyman, was later to die in a mental hospital—and, in
1919, Felkin was forced to close the Temple down.

The Stella Matutina seem to have originally derived their
spiritualistic interpretation—or rather misinterpretation—of the
Golden Dawn's techniques of astral projection and travel, from
Florence Farr's 'Sphere', but they indulged in them to a far
greater extent. There were two main groups of the 'astral
entities' contacted. The first group was Rosicrucian and, at times,
the medium was believed to be controlled by the spirit of Christian Rosycross himself! The second were 'Arabs'—they claimed
to be the original teachers of Christian Rosycross—and were
led by a spirit called Ara ben Shemesh, who described himself[1]
as coming 'from the Temple in the Desert, and those who live
there are the Sons of Fire. There are three ranks—Neophytes or
Catechumens; the Accepted and Proven; and the Indwellers.
The last are those we call Masters. They live in personal communion with the Divine, and being no longer bound in the
flesh, their material life is entirely a matter of will. So long

---

[1] At a seance, probably taking place in the 'Vault of the Adepti', held on
January 26th, 1909.

as they are required as teachers, so long may they continue to inhabit the earthly tabernacle. When they have completed their task they will dematerialise. Christian Rosycross came to us and learnt much. From us he took the letters C.R., the true interpretation of which is one of the great mysteries of the universe.'

In the Stella Matutina History Lecture, written by Mrs. Felkin, exalted claims were made as to the nature and value of the teachings received from these astral sources:

> The Hidden Order ... is always secret and hidden, the Masters from time to time select one or two to send out as teachers when the world is ready for them.... Such teachers gather round the inner secret Orders, and, to members of these who are found worthy, messengers from the hidden Masters are sent to give them teaching, not materially, but on the astral plane.
>
> If the pupils have courage, patience, perseverance, and loyalty to follow this teaching, and to practice the methods, the time will come when they will receive direct instructions from the hidden Masters, either singly or in groups; and it may be that the pupils will eventually be led to one of the great secret hidden Temples that are here and there in the world. We, your Chiefs, can say that we know this to our own knowledge, because we have thus received and visited. It is in your power to do as we have done, but it requires patience, faith, self sacrifice, and the ordering of the outer life before the inner teaching can be received. There must be sacrifice, and you must be ready to give up even your own will at times and eliminate much work and pleasure which others may seem to enjoy.

The 'great, secret, hidden Temple' which Mrs. Felkin and her fellow-Chiefs claimed to have visited, existed only on the astral plane, and was divided into twenty-two chapels, representing the twelve Zodiacal signs, the seven planets known to the ancients, and the elements of fire, water and air. 'Ara ben Shemesh' described the functions of these chapels in a mediumistic communication received on November 11th, 1911:

Each chapel foreshadows a life force which we are now to begin to experience. We have been putting together as it were the ingredients, and now the FIRE has to be lit, and the ingredients are to be boiled down.

The orders given by the 'Arab teacher' had a considerable effect on the Stella Matutina's policies. The following instruction for example, received on January 9th, 1915, was eventually put into effect by the foundation of the Anglican spiritual healing organisation called the Guild of St. Raphael,[2] the founders of which were, almost without exception, members of the Stella Matutina:

The alternative training for those whom we were speaking of should be definitely fixed now and put on the same footing as the Daughter Temples, as a special group for healing. It should be called the Healers or Therapeutae, and [Father X][3] should be made specially and definitely the head of it, and those who wish to follow that training should be taken from all the different Temples and kept in touch with one another.

The outbreak of the War in 1914 seems to have taken both the Felkins and their astral teachers by surprise—for the former were still in Germany in August 1914 (as usual they had been visiting Rosicrucian Temples), and only managed to get out of that country with the aid of their high-grade masonic friends. Nevertheless, 'Ara ben Shemesh' had his own theories about the war, which he said was '... an inevitable means of destroying the old order of things to make room for the new; that already the ideas of peace and unity have been implanted, but they could not spread freely until the old had been broken asunder. It is the "Tower struck by Lightning"—the "Rending Asunder of the Veil".'

[2] The Guild of St. Raphael is still extremely active today, but I have no reason to think that its present-day leadership is in any way concerned with the magical arts.

[3] Here I omit the name of a 'Mirfield Father'—a member of the Anglican Community of the Resurrection.

Vitality is being forced into action just now, and the reaction will be complete depletion, unless those who are not actually taking part in the conflict store up a power to be set free as soon as the conflict ceases. Not only our own group, but all those we know of should be instructed to devote themselves to this aim ... the human spirit seeks to free itself from earth and rise to the greatest heights of which it is capable ... but the human brain is like the transmitter of a wireless station ... and for every aspiration there is a reply.... A man praying to the devil enters into the communion of evil, but he also formulates the evil forces which react upon all those who are not positively in search of the good. For you must never forget that any force which can be contacted through such prayer is not only a negative receiver but also a positive transmitter which sends out its currents and vibrations to all those who are capable of receiving them.

From 1916 onwards Miss Stoddart (Soror Het-ta), the ruling Chief of Amoun Temple and her two clerical co-Chiefs, engaged themselves almost non-stop in these astral junkettings. The extract that follows is a typical example of the sort of visions they saw.

A dark room with dark, polished floor and dark walls. People sitting round a dark polished table. An old man sitting at the head in a carved arm-chair. There are lights in sconces round the walls reflected on the polished floor. All are in dark robes; the old man has a curious cap, not unlike that of the Jewish High Priest, curved up at the sides like horns. It is red, embroidered with gold and jewels. A brazier is in the centre of the table; every now and then someone casts a little incense on it. Each has a dish of incense before him, each of a different kind, and they all sprinkle in turn. The seat at the foot of the table, similar to that at the head, is vacant, so thirteen in all. There are six people on either side of the table. The old man is speaking. He has bright dark eyes with rather drooping lids. He seems to say: 'The time is approaching and we are not yet fully prepared. I must remain here to keep the fire burning, but you must return, each to his own country, and when we gather here again the vacant chair will be filled.' They all make a sign with the left hand, as if they quickly draw a line with it on the right hand which was held with the fingers stiffly together, the right elbow resting on the table. They have deeply engraved seal rings on the first finger, large dark stones. We may meet the one that is to come back to this country. It is difficult to see the faces, as they wear dominoes with hoods pulled over their heads. Now all are standing up and repeating a Latin verse. First something in unison—I John iv. 7-12. Then each says a word in turn from one of the texts. The man that is to come here says 'Amor'. Then together they say, 'Nobis hoc signum'. The old man looks Italian or Jewish.... It is very mountainous outside.... He is standing now, and has stepped to the side of his chair, which seems to be on two steps, so that he is level with the table. The people file past him and each gives a grip and a password. This password seems to be the word from each that was said in the sentence. They line up at a curtained door and face him. He has a heavy gold cross around his neck with which he blesses them. They make a gesture like a salaam and disappear behind the curtain. On the table before the old man's seat is a black ebony lotus wand. The lotus is closed to form a cone; it has a light round it. The old man is left alone; he goes round the table and puts the remains of the incense from each dish on to the brazier. Now he takes off his curious cap and sets it on the table beside the wand. He takes off his domino, he is looking very thoughtful. He is not more than fifty-five or sixty, has a silky dark beard, dark moustache, dark hair parting in the middle, curling and just showing thin on the top. He has got on a cassock. Now he is picking up his wand; he presses a little knob in the handle of it and the flower falls open. The flower is of mother-of-pearl with a shining crystal centre. It is flat, but sparkles in the light. He is saying something in a foreign language about the Law: 'The Law shall be fulfilled'.

From the beginning of 1917 onwards there was an absolute

flood of these visions, accompanied by messages about, and instructions designed to achieve, a coming 'Great Initiation'. To prepare for this event the three London Chiefs were instructed to form a so-called 'triangle of power' which would form a link with the 'hidden Masters'. The three Chiefs were told that they were: 'The three chosen for my work. Ye are the Love, the Power, and the Perfect Reconciliation, and to ye shall come the Perfect Unity.... The day of disintegration and death lieth indeed before you, but fear it not, ye have passed beyond the harming power of death and only the final test remains. Unharmed and unhurt shall ye pass the barrier, the veil is thinning, urge ever upwards to the Light.'

Miss Stoddart herself was told that she was to be the 'apex of the Triangle, and ye must first pass within the veil, that from the apex may shine down the glorious beauty from the Father's face. In pure spirit must ye work upon the earth, for ye are a reflection of that brightness and purity which ever burns within the flame.'

She was also instructed to join the Anglican Church—after all, her two colleagues were Church of England clergymen—which she accordingly did; the experiences she underwent during Church services, however, were not those normally associated with membership of the eminently-sane body. For she went into trances, saw visions, and received much astral teaching!

The culmination of all these peculiar happenings took place at an Easter service, held on April 17th, 1919, at which Miss Stoddart saw, in place of the altar, the Vault of the Adepti, into which filed twelve black-robed and cowled figures. She then felt a sharp pain in her heart, followed by what she described as a 'curious creeping faintness'. These phenomena were accompanied, so she said, by a dazzling fire above her head. Next day her 'hidden Master' informed her that her failure to achieve the 'Great Initiation' was due to a mistake and that it would be satisfactorily completed in the future. By this time, however, both she and her fellow-schizophrenics had decided that the experiences they were undergoing—astral attacks, mysterious smells, visions of the astral light, spontaneous trance—were caused by 'Black Rosicrucians' who were trying to achieve con-

trol of their physical bodies. Accordingly they sent a cable to
Felkin in New Zealand begging for his help. Even Felkin, a man
who seems to have been usually incapable of the ordinary processes of rational thought, sensed that something was seriously
wrong with the minds of his Chiefs, for he wrote:

> Such attacks as those you have had are quite definitely an
> attempt of evil forces to distract the soul in its ascent of the
> Mountain. So soon as this is accomplished the attacks cease.
> They are in themselves a proof that the teaching receiver is
> both good and highly important.
> I think it would be better if, instead of fearing imaginary
> Black Rosicrucians in Germany or elsewhere, you would
> consciously endeavour to co-operate with the true Rosicru-
> cians who do undoubtedly exist, and are seeking to guide
> Central European thought into the Light; you would then
> belong to the Great Work for the world.

The recipients of this letter were unconvinced and the Amoun
Temple, mother-Temple of the Stella Matutina, was closed down.
The mad clergyman went off to what was then called the
lunatic asylum, and there, in the course of time, he died. Not
so Miss Stoddart; she became a sort of jingoistic proto-fascist,
convinced of the genuineness of the 'Protocols of the Learned
Elders of Zion', convinced that the Golden Dawn, the Stella
Matutina, and all other magical fraternities were agents of a
Jewish world-conspiracy, and sure that secret societies were
the sole cause of world-unrest! For years she wrote a fortnightly
column for the *Patriot*, under the nom-de-plume of 'Inquire
Within'—later selections from it were reprinted as *Lightbearers
of Darkness*—which makes hilarious reading today. It is interesting to note, in view of later history, that she believed that
German nationalism and the German General Staff were mere
agents of the Jewish plan for world-conquest!

CHAPTER FIFTEEN

The Cromlech Temple

As far as I know, there is not a single printed reference to the Cromlech Temple, an esoteric group, having a close fraternal relationship and many members in common with the Golden Dawn, which produced some extremely interesting papers on the significance of the higher Rosicrucian grades in general and that of Exempt Adept in particular.

In one of its Knowledge Lectures the Cromlech Temple claimed that 'our traditions go back almost to the time of the Master Jesus', in another it claimed St. Theresa of Ávila as a member. An occultist tells me that in their highest sense he believes these statements to be true; 'for every effective mystical group is part of the Great Order behind all earthly orders, a link in that great shining chain of Prophets, Priests and Magi which we can faintly discern as it runs backward through time until lost in the mists of pre-history'. In the purely mundane historical sense, however, the Order seems to have originated at some time between 1890 and 1910, probably in Scotland, and its rituals seem to have derived from those of the dormant Masonic body the Sat B'hai, but with the symbolism transformed from that of the Vedas to that of the religion of ancient Iran. In spite of the Zoroastrian form of these rituals their inner content was a high, mystical, and authentically Gnostic interpretation of Christianity.

It was not until after the First World War that the Cromlech Temple began to expand rapidly. Numerous Anglo-Catholic clergymen were attracted by the Order's Gnostic interpretations of such High Anglican doctrines as the Immaculate Conception and the 'three-branch' theory of the Universal Church. Another attraction for any young Priest fearful of drifting into some form of non-Christian illuminism was the fact that only convinced Christians could be admitted into grades beyond the first—and even in this preliminary grade the candidate was required to express his belief in some form of monotheism.

The Christian bias of the Order is well conveyed by the following extract from one of its Second Grade papers:

> We believe that we have been able to preserve all the pure doctrines of the Catholic Church and to know and reject those that have been introduced by corruption, or for material and political ends. Our Order then—meaning the governing and teaching body, is absolutely within the Church. Yet we do not refuse to teach the Neophytes of any other faith. Only they cannot advance to higher grades unless they be Christians and members of one of the branches of the Catholic Church.

Most of the new members came in directly from the ordinary ecclesiastical world and had had no previous contact with any organisation giving ritual initiation. The Cromlech Temple itself did not practice Ceremonial Magic—its rituals were largely confined to its initiations, an extremely Christianised version of the Qabalistic Cross, a ritual known as the consecration of the Golden Ark, and the Mystical Adoration of the Quipus, a cord of seven colours worn as part of the Lodge regalia—and many of the new entrants desired to learn the traditional magical skills of Western Occultism.

These would-be Adepti were advised to get their practical training from the Golden Dawn; an addendum to the MS given to all entrants to the Second (Eagle) Grade said:

> If you seek for practical instruction in the Occult Arts or Sciences mentioned in the Ritual of this grade instructions may be obtained through the Society of the Golden and Rosy Cross known as the A.O. in the Outer. With the knowledge and training obtained in the higher grades thereof it will be possible for each of you, if ye advance far enough, to communicate personally with the Masters of this Order. And there

135

are good and sufficient reasons why we should direct you to study in this Society rather than give instructions ourselves.

It is clear that some relationship also existed between the Cromlech Temple and the Stella Matutina, for amongst the documents circulating in the former group was one entitled the 'Veils of Negative Existence', purporting to be an English translation of an Arab work of the sixth, seventh or eighth centuries, and Felkin gave a lecture on this work to the Study Group of the Metropolitan College of the Societa Rosicruciana in Anglia on January 11th, 1915.[1]

To me it seems unquestionable that the Cromlech Temple was correct in its decision to leave the teaching of Ritual Magic to the Golden Dawn, for, quite apart from the duplication of effort involved, its chiefs seem to have had little talent for the construction of Rituals. Their Christian reconstruction of the Qabalistic Cross, for example, was markedly inferior to the original.

Although specifically Christian the Cromlech Temple's version of that faith was far from exclusive and it taught that there were many other Paths to the Highest. Some extracts from one of the Order's Second Grade papers makes its attitude clear.

Consider now the Master's own words: 'Other sheep have I which are not of this fold.' ... 'Feed my sheep.' Brother in these words of His the Master speaks to thee. Now look back and see how thee thyself hast drawn nigh unto Him. It was by one of the most perfect expressions of His Divine Spirit, the formularies of the Catholic Church. This was the step that lay before thee and though didst mount thereon and find the Lord.

Highly privileged wert thou for there is no other road whereby so rapidly or so nearly may approach to Him be won. This step is a White Stone—but if thou sholdst make a fetich thereof as the Moslems do of their Kaaba and say

---

[1] The authoress of *Light Bearers of Darkness* also refers to an Edinburgh Sun Order, which may possibly bear some relationship to the Cromlech Temple. I think it far more likely, however, that the so-called Edinburgh Sun Order was a group of 'astral masters' contacted by Brodie-Innes.

there is no other way, thou wouldst gravely err. For herein do men often confound what is useful discipline and of immense value to them who are at the stage to profit thereby with the absolute essential of the Master's teaching and the New Revelation.

These limitations are easy and therefore dear to the human hearts of human teachers—very easy it is to say 'My way is the only way, walk ye in it'. Very hard to see the way that lies before another and to aid him to walk in the path that the Master has traced before him—much easier to force him to walk in thy path. Much easier, but not the Master's method. Forbid him not because he walketh not with you.'

Thou shouldst call nothing common or unclean. That man or woman who seeks a good or fancied good, be it what it may, even if it be merely sensual lust (which to him or her seems the best thing), is all unknown to himself or herself seeking him the Master; the soul is young, the ideal is low and primitive, but nevertheless it is an ideal—by degrees other ideals will be substituted for the lower ones—'Feed my lambs' said the Master, not drive them into your own favourite pasture.

Nothing is common or unclean—the sacrifice he asks of thee is the sacrifice of thy prejudices, thy limitations, in order that thou mayest feed his sheep, above all his lambs.

Well canst thou guide members of the Catholic Church in Catholic ways. This is easy and demands no sacrifice. Thou art asked to see his hand everywhere—to recognise that faiths thou callest heathen may have a knowledge of Him. That there are grains of Truth everywhere—that thou art called to be a shepherd.

This shows a far more tolerant and sophisticated attitude towards 'sensual lust' than one would expect from a body consisting largely of Anglican clergy; in fact the Order's tolerance was extended to all that is normally regarded as evil[2] and

[2] This tolerance was not, needless to say, extended to a deliberate descent into Qlipothic evil, a conscious saying of 'evil be thou my good', a search after that Abyss of Ecstatic Evil which is the inversion of the Saints' Ecstacy of Good.

this unusual attitude is more fully developed in another Order document:

> For ye know that the Master needeth not only all whom the world calls good and holy, but that those whom the world calls evil are a part of His Body and move with His Will—the outer and uninitiated unconsciously, the Adept consciously and willingly. The Pharisees and Scribes despised Mary Magdalene, the woman who was a sinner, yet was she at that time developing towards the high Adeptship to which she afterwards attained. She yielded herself willingly through her love to be a vessel, whether of honour or dishonour, in her Master's hands.
>
> Few can attain to this height but one lesson ye can learn of infinite importance in this Fire Tattva. Any person soever ye may see may for aught you know be on the Path of Adeptiship and in love yielding himself to the Master's will, though seeming evil to you as Mary Magdalene seemed to the Pharisees, therefore condemn not and ye shall not be condemned.

Also interesting in this connection were the Cromlech Temple's teachings on love and sexuality.[3]

In the Third Grade was taught a method of obtaining what some mystics have called detachment and the Cromlech Temple called Negative Vision. While the method was by no means completely original (it resembles many traditional techniques including certain exercises of Hatha Yoga) there are some quite interesting points in the relevant Order document:

> ... the negative sight is not self regarding. It makes no impression on us. The passing show passes before our eyes merely as might the pictures of a cinematograph. It interests us, it may excite us to a certain extent. It may teach us lessons, but it does not affect us further than this. Now the Adept habitually looks thus at the things within his sight.

[3] See Appendix F.

He knows when it is wise and right that he should be affected, and otherwise he does not permit himself to be affected. If it is right that he should be affected he can at will produce the positive sight and see the thing in relation to himself— calling on him for action or sympathy or whatsoever is right and wise. With this Negative sight he sees not only the passing show, but he sees the reasons and moving causes behind and can often discern the good in seeming evil, the Angels working behind what appears to be diabolic. I mean he can actually see the one as clearly as the other, though both are to some extent dreamy and insubstantial. His wisdom here is therefore truer and he rejoices where with the Positive sight he might grieve, or be indignant or nauseated.

To attain the Negative sight needs for many people practice....

To rouse this Negative vision in one who has never experienced it, the head should be perfectly still and the muscles of the neck relaxed, therefore it is best that the head be supported behind and the whole attitude easy, the head being somewhat thrown back, so that the line of the eyes is directed a little above the horizon line.

Now endeavour to hold the eyes perfectly still, not looking at anything but just waiting for what may pass before them. Draw in the breath gently, almost imperceptibly, and at the same time slightly raise the eyebrows and eyelids letting the head sink very, very slightly backwards.

The sensation should be as though the eyeballs were sinking slightly into the head, and a dreamy feeling will come over, there will be no desire to look at anything, but observe whatever comes, and an entire indifference to what it may be. There will be neither sorrow nor joy at what is seen, there will be an admiration at whatever passes, and a recognition of seeing the wonderful works of God. Nothing seen will possibly move the seer to action. He will be as a scientist observing through his microscope....

The exercise should not at first be prolonged, but it may be often repeated, and with each repetition will become easier, until he is able to produce this type of vision at will, even

139

when walking along the road, or in the street, or wherever he may be.

All things considered, the Cromlech Temple was an interesting side-Order to the Golden Dawn and as will be seen in a later Chapter, it is directly responsible for two authentic Golden Dawn Temples still operating at the present time.

As I have previously said, it is most surprising that no mention of it seems to have got into print.

Additional Note A good many of the Cromlech Temple's instructional manuscripts have now been printed; they are to be found in *Astral Projection, Ritual Magic and Alchemy* (Aquarian, 1987).

CHAPTER SIXTEEN

Mrs. Mathers Accused of Murder!

MacGregor Mathers died in 1918, a casualty of that world-wide influenza epidemic whose victims numbered more than those of the Somme, second Mons, and the other great blood-lettings of the First World War. He was succeeded by his widow, Moina Mathers, who carried on the Alpha et Omega in co-operation with the now-ageing Brodie-Innes. Alas, however, the 'mantle of Elijah did not descend on Mrs. Elisha', and Mrs. Mathers governed the Order in an erratic and, at times, unintelligent manner. One of her more extraordinary actions is referred to by Regardie in his *My Rosicrucian Adventure*—she gave permission to the Chief of an American Temple to conduct a correspondence course at the conclusion of which pupils were 'initiated' by post in return for a fee of ten dollars!

Following this there was a rapid mushrooming in the number of American Temples and, while the number of genuine Adepti grew less and less, there was a vast increase in the numbers of those who combined magical ineptitude with high-sounding titles and grades. Several initiates, disgusted by this unsatisfactory state of affairs, broke away and formed independent Temples and groups which continued to teach the Golden Dawn system —although not usually in its entirety. Typical of these was the 'School of Ageless Wisdom' (founded by Paul Foster Case and surviving to the present day as the 'Builders of the Adytum Ltd.') which did not, for example, use the original Golden Dawn designs of the Tarot cards but instead adopted a modified version

141

of the pack designed by A. E. Waite.[1]

Perhaps the major problem Mrs. Mathers had to face in the 'twenties was her relationship with the young psychic and occultist Violet Firth. The latter, who later married a Dr. Evans, but is best known by her pen-name of Dion Fortune, was initiated as a Neophyte of the Alpha et Omega in 1919. Although still young she had been fascinated by the occult tradition for as long as she could remember, and, while still in her 'teens, had developed marked mediumistic powers which had caused some excitement in the small country town where she was living.

At first she was a member of what she referred to as 'the Southern branch of the Scottish section of the Order'—in other words an English Temple operating under the general overlordship of Brodie-Innes—but in 1920 she transferred to a London Temple working directly under the rule of Mathers' widow. Mrs. Mathers, usually known to her fellow-Hermeticists as Vestigia, was impressed by the energy of the slim[2] young girl, for Violet approached the magical arts with the same enthusiasm that she gave to the rest of her many and varied interests; these included the problem of purity, the psychology of the servant problem, and the soya bean as an article of diet, on all of which subjects she was to write books within a short space of time!

Dion Fortune—it is perhaps best to use the name by which she wished to be known—was impressed by the Golden Dawn teachings but not by the way they were taught in the Alpha et Omega. She wrote: 'Practical teaching from official sources was conspicuous by its absence, and unless one was lucky enough to have a personal friend amongst its members with a gift of exposition, one was left high and dry. One was put through the ceremonies, given the bare bones of the system in the knowledge

[1] It is often thought that the pack designed under Waite's supervision contain the authentic Golden Dawn designs but there are, in fact, several major variations. In the Waite pack, for example, ATU VI illustrates a rather anaemic angel blessing a naked man and woman while the Golden Dawn card shows Perseus and Andromeda, the latter chained to a rock, the former flying with drawn sword to her assistance.

[2] Later she was to become very fat; for some reason most mediums seem to do this—probably there is some relationship between mediumship and the glandular balance of the metabolism.

lectures and a few commentaries on them called side-lectures, for the most part of very inferior quality, and left to one's own devices.' She felt that the Order needed new blood, that it was manned 'mainly by widows and grey-bearded ancients', and she came to the conclusion that this end could best be achieved by organising a public or semi-public society to act as an outer court to the Golden Dawn system, a sort of magically orientated Theosophical Society which would arrange public meetings, organise lectures, issue a magazine etc.

She approached her Chief with this proposal and, surprisingly enough (for previously Mrs. Mathers had shared her husband's passion for secrecy), it was accepted. Thus, in 1922, the Fraternity of the Inner Light came into existence—although for a considerable time it acted under the guise of the 'Christian Mystic Lodge of the Theosophical Society'—and through its work a trickle of new recruits began to come into the Golden Dawn. These were welcomed eagerly by Mrs. Mathers, who had by now become an enthusiastic Empire-builder, prepared to sacrifice quality for quantity,[3] but she soon became aware that in the Fraternity of the Inner Light, Dion Fortune, already beginning to indulge in much astral travel, getting trance messages from Masters of the Western Tradition etc., was beginning to build up a little Empire of her own.

Mrs. Mathers took appropriate action and tried to expel Dion Fortune for 'betraying the inner secrets of the Order' in her book *Esoteric Philosophy of Love and Marriage*, but later forgave her 'when it was pointed out to Vestigia that Dion Fortune had not yet achieved the grade in which this teaching was given'. This whole episode puzzles me, for I can find little resemblance between the wishy-washy, semi-spiritualist meanderings of *Esoteric Philosophy of Love and Marriage*, probably Dion Fortune's worst book, and any aspect of the Order's teaching.

A little later Mrs Mathers took strong objection to a series of articles that her erstwhile favourite published in the *Occult*

[3] In 1926 her introduction to a new edition of one of her husband's works not only referred to the esoteric school founded by her husband, but intimated that admission to it could be obtained by writing to her c/o the Publisher. A pamphlet issued by her in the United States was, I believe, even more explicit.

Review—they were later republished under the title of *Sane Occultism*—and first suspended and finally expelled her (on the grounds that certain symbols had not appeared in her aura) from the Order.

Dion Fortune persisted in using the Order system and set up a Temple of her own which had a semi-amicable relationship with the surviving Temples of the Stella Matutina. Mrs. Mathers met this defiance by using Black Magic and launching a psychic attack on the rebel—or so, at any rate, Dion Fortune believed. Whether they were objective or subjective, the experiences undergone by Dion Fortune were most unpleasant. She described them as follows:

... My first intimation of it was a sense of uneasiness and restlessness. Next came a feeling as if the barriers between the Seen and the Unseen were full of rifts and I kept on getting glimpses of the astral mingling with my waking consciousness. This, for me, is unaccustomed, for I am not naturally psychic, and in the technique in which I was trained we are taught to keep the different levels of consciousness strictly separate and to use a specific method for opening and closing the gates. Consequently one seldom gets spontaneous psychism. One's vision resembles the use of a microscope in which one examines prepared material.

The general sense of vague uneasiness gradually matured into a definite sense of menace and antagonism, and presently I began to see demon faces in flashes, resembling those picture-images which psychologists call by the unpleasing name of hypnagogics, flashes of dream which appear upon the threshold of sleep. I was quite unsuspicious of any particular individual, though I realised that my articles had probably stirred somebody up pretty thoroughly; what was my surprise, then, to receive from a person whom I looked upon as a friend and for whom I had the greatest respect, a letter which left me in no doubt whatever as to the source of the attack and what I might expect if any more articles were published. I can honestly say that until I received this letter I had not the slightest suspicion that this person was implicated in the scandals I was attacking.

I was in a somewhat difficult position; I had fired off a charge of shrapnel on general principles, and had apparently 'bagged' a number of my friends and associates and fluttered the dove-cote generally. My position was rather complicated by the fact that I did not know nearly as much as they apparently suspected me of doing; I had, of course, known that these abuses existed sporadically about the occult field as everybody in the movement knows; but to know in this vague way is one thing, and to put one's finger on specific cases is another. I had evidently blundered into something much more considerable than I had bargained for. I felt like the small boy who, fishing for minnows, has hooked a pike. I had to decide whether I would try and get my articles back from the *Occult Review*, or whether I would let them run their natural course and take the consequences. I had had a very strong impulse to write those articles, and now I began to see why I had had it. I shall have something to say in another chapter concerning the Watchers, that curious section of the Occult Hierarchy which is concerned with the welfare of nations. A certain section of their work is apparently concerned with the policing of the Astral Plane. Very little is actually known about them. One comes across their work sporadically and pieces the bits together. I have crossed their trail on several occasions, as I will tell later. Whenever black magic is afoot, they set to work to put a spoke in its wheels. Be that as it may. I came to the conclusion that, in view of what had now transpired, the impulse I had had to take in hand this piece of work might have emanated from the Watchers. At any rate, the work obviously needed doing. Someone had to tackle these plague spots if they were to be cleared up, so I determined to stick to my guns and see the matter through, and so left the articles in question to run their course.

Very soon some curious things began to happen. We became most desperately afflicted with black cats. They were not hallucinatory cats, for our neighbours shared in the affliction, and we exchanged commiserations with the caretaker next door who was engaged in pushing bunches of black cats off doorstep and window-sill with a broom, and declared he had never in his life seen so many, or such dreadful specimens. The whole house was filled with the horrible stench of the brutes. Two members of our community at that time went out to business every day, and at their offices, in different parts of London, they found the same penetrating reek of the tom-cat.

At first we attributed this persecution to natural causes, and concluded that we were near neighbours of some fascinating feline female, but incidents succeeded each other which made us feel that things were not quite in the ordinary course of nature. We were getting near to the Vernal Equinox, which is always a difficult time for occultists; there was a sense of strain and tension in the atmosphere, and we were all feeling decidedly uncomfortable. Coming upstairs after breakfast one morning, I suddenly saw, coming down the stairs towards me, a gigantic tabby cat, twice the size of a tiger. It appeared absolutely solid and tangible. I stared at it petrified for a second, and then it vanished. I instantly realised that it was a simulacrum, or thought-form that was being projected by someone with occult powers. Not that the realisation was any too comforting, but it was better than an actual tiger. Feeling decidedly uncomfortable, I asked one of my household to join me, and as we sat in my room meditating we heard the cry of a cat from without. It was answered by another, and another. We looked out of the window, and the street as far as we could see was dotted with black cats and they were wailing and howling in broad daylight as they do on the roofs at night.

I rose up, gathered together my paraphernalia, and did an exorcism then and there. At the end we looked out of the window again. The visitation was at an end. Only our normal population of local mousers remained to us.

The Vernal Equinox was now upon us. I must explain that this is the most important season of the year for occultists. Great power-tides are flowing on the Inner Planes, and these are very difficult to handle. If there is going to be astral trouble, it usually blows up for a storm at this season. There are also certain meetings which take place on the Astral Plane, and many occultists attend them out of the body. In order to do this, one has to throw oneself into a trance and then the mind is free to travel. It is usual to get someone who understands these mehods of work to watch beside the body while it is vacated to see that it comes to no harm.

In the ordinary way, when an occult attack is afoot, one clings to waking consciousness at all costs, sleeping by day and keeping awake and meditating while the sun is below the horizon. As ill-luck would have it, however, I was obliged to make one of these astral journeys at this season. My attacker knew this as well as I did. I therefore made my preparations with all the precautions I could think of; gathered together a carefully chosen group to form the watching circle, and sealed up the place of operation with the usual ceremonial. I had not much faith in this operation under the circumstances, for my attacker was of much higher grade than I was, and could come through any seals I might set. However, it afforded protection against minor unpleasantness.

The method of making these astral journeys is highly technical, and I cannot enter upon it here. In the language of psychology, it is auto-hypnosis by means of a symbol. The symbol acts as a door to the Unseen. According to the symbol chosen will be the section of the Unseen to which access is obtained. The trained initiate, therefore, does not wander on the astral like an uneasy ghost, but comes and goes by well-known corridors.

My enemy's task was therefore not a difficult one; for she knew about the time I must make this journey and the symbol I must use in order to get out of the body. I was therefore prepared for opposition, though I did not know what form it would take.

These astral journeys are really lucid dreams in which one retains all one's faculties of choice, will-power and judgment. Mine always begin with a curtain of the symbolic colour through whose folds I pass. No sooner was I through the curtain on this occasion than I saw my enemy waiting for

147

me, or, if another terminology is preferred, I began to dream about her. She appeared to me in the full robes of her grade, which were very magnificent, and barred my entry, telling me that by virtue of her authority she forbade me to make use of these astral pathways. I replied that I did not admit her right to close the astral paths to me because she was personally offended, and that I appealed to the Inner Chiefs, to whom both she and I were responsible. Then ensued a battle of wills in which I experienced the sensation of being whirled through the air and falling from a great height and found myself back in my body. But my body was not where I had left it, but in a heap in the far corner of the room, which looked as if it had been bombed. By means of the well-known prenomenon of repercussion the astral struggle had apparently communicated itself to the body, which had somersaulted round the room while an agitated group had rescued the furniture from its path.

I was somewhat shaken by this experience, which had not been a pleasant one. I recognised that I had had the worst of it and had been effectually ejected from the astral paths; but I also realised that if I accepted this defeat my occult career was at an end. Just as a child who has been thrown by his pony must immediately get up and remount if he is ever to ride again, so I knew that at all costs I must make that astral journey if I were to retain my powers. So I told my group to pull themselves together and re-form the circle because we must make another attempt; I invoked the Inner Chiefs, and went out once more. This time there was a short sharp struggle, and I was through. I had the Vision of the Inner Chiefs, and returned. The fight was over. I have never had any trouble since.

But when I took off my clothes in order to go to bed my back felt very sore, and taking a hand-glass I examined it in the mirror, and I found that from neck to waist I was scored with scratches as if I had been clawed by a gigantic cat.

I told this story to some friends of mine, experienced occultists, who at one time had been closely associated with the person with whom I had had this trouble, and they told me that she was well-known for these astral attacks, and that a friend of theirs after a quarrel with her had an exactly similar experience, and she too had been covered with claw-marks. In her case, however, she had been ill for six months and had never touched occultism again.[4]

Elsewhere Dion Fortune actually accused Mrs. Mathers of the psychic murder of Miss Netta Fornario, a member of the Alpha et Omega, who had died in unusual and mysterious circumstances.

The alleged murder-victim, who had an Italian father (whom she hated) and an English mother, was in appearance a typical member of the arts-and-crafts movement, wearing hand-woven silken or woollen tunics, and dressing her dark hair in two heavy plaits.

In the autumn of 1929, when she was about thirty-five years of age, she left her London home and travelled to the 'Holy Isle' of Iona, situated off the western coast of Scotland, taking with her a large amount of luggage, which included packing cases containing sufficient furniture to fully equip a small house —clearly she intended her stay in Iona to be a lengthy one. For the moment, however, she boarded with Mrs. MacRae, a native of the island, who fascinated her lodger with stories of mysterious happenings and the folklore of the Hebrides. Mrs. MacRae was equally fascinated by her guest whom she suspected of indulging in what she was later to call 'mystical practices'. Her fascination turned to alarm, however, when Miss Fornario told her that she had recently undergone a trance lasting a full week and thought that there was a strong possibility that she might again undergo such a trance in the near future—under no circumstances, added Miss Fornario, was Mrs. MacRae to call a physician.

One Sunday morning, some two months after she had arrived on Iona, Miss Fornario got up very early—a marked break in

---

[4] It will be noted that in this quotation Dion Fortune merely describes her opponent as 'a person I looked upon as a friend'; but in her article 'Ceremonial Magic Unveiled' (*Occult Review*, Jan. 1933) she clearly identifies this 'friend' with Mrs. Mathers.

her routine, for normally she lay in bed until eleven. She seemed
to be in a panic-stricken state and told her landlady that she
had to make an immediate departure for London; she added that
'certain people' were affecting her telepathically and went on
to talk in a disjointed way of a 'rudderless boat that went across
the sky' and 'messages she had received from other worlds'. Mrs.
MacRae was disturbed by this and her Highland superstitions
were amused by the fact that, overnight, Miss Fornario's silver
jewellery had turned completely black.[5]

At that time it was impossible to get a boat to Mull on a
Sunday—it is not particularly easy today—and Miss Fornario
spent the day packing her belongings. Suddenly she changed
her mind; she retired to her room for a short time and then
came out with what was later described as 'a calm look of
resignation on her face', telling her hostess that she had decided
to cancel her departure and would now remain indefinitely on
Iona.

On the following morning Miss Fornario was missing from her
room. At first Mrs. MacRae was not unduly alarmed and
thought that her guest was simply taking an early walk along
the beach, but as the day wore on her fears were aroused and
a search was made of the nearby moors and beach.

Some two and a half miles from the cottage were the remains
of an ancient village in which Miss Fornario had displayed a
strong interest. She had never visited it, however, for access
was difficult, the site being surrounded by rocks on three sides
and by moor and peat-bog on the other. It was within half a
mile of this village that, on the Tuesday, her dead body was
found.

Except for the black cloak of the Hiereus (an important officer in a Golden Dawn Temple) the body was naked. Round
its neck was a blackened silver chain, in its hand was a large

[5] It would be interesting to know whether Miss Fornario was a vegetarian
and, if so, whether eggs formed a considerable part of her diet. My friend
Gillian Dutfield, expert on modern gold and silver jewellery and owner of
those two delightful browsing places called Craft Gallery, tells me that
she has known vegetarians whose sweat contains such a high percentage of
sulphur compounds (derived from eggs) that silver jewellery would turn
black on them within half-an-hour of it being donned.

steel knife, the soles of its feet were torn and had bled heavily although the heels were intact—clearly Miss Fornario had ran for a considerable distance before she had come to her stopping place and cut into the turf the large cross, on which, so the examining physician said, she had met her death by heart failure.

The *Occult Review* (Jan. 1930) briefly reported the death as follows:

The mysterious death of a student of occultism, Miss N. Fornario, is receiving the attention of the authorities at the present time. Miss Fornario was found lying nude on the bleak hill-side in the lonely island of Iona. Round her neck was a cross secured by a silver chain, and near at hand lay a large knife which had been used to cut a large cross in the turf. On this cross her body was lying. A resident of London, Miss Fornario seems to have made her way to Iona for some purpose connected with occultism. One of the servants at her house in London stated that a letter had been received saying she had a 'terrible case of healing on'. One newspaper report alludes to 'mysterious stories on the island about blue lights having been seen in the vicinity of where her body was found, and there is also a story of a cloaked man'. Occultists no less than the general public will await with interest any disclosures that may be forthcoming concerning this occurrence.

I think it certain that either Miss Fornario was the victim of some sort of magical attack, or, and most people will believe this to be the more probable explanation, was suffering from an acute attack of schizophrenia and believed herself subjected to such an attack.

Dion Fortune had no doubts on the matter, for, after reproducing the above brief quotation from the *Occult Review*, she stated that the body was scratched, that Miss Fornario had been associated with Mrs. Mathers, and that victims of the latter's alleged 'astral attacks' always have the marks of scratches.

CHAPTER SEVENTEEN

Regardie and His Impact

Francis Israel Regardie was born in England on November 17th, 1907 but, when only thirteen years old, he emigrated to the U.S.A. and must therefore be regarded as an American. While still a young student he came across the writings of C. S. Jones and some volumes of Crowley's *Equinox*; he immediately became fascinated by the magical tradition, the Golden Dawn, and perhaps most of all, the extraordinary personality of Aleister Crowley.

So great was the fascination that, in 1928, he travelled to Europe and became Crowley's unpaid secretary-companion—Crowley nicknamed his amanuensis 'the Serpent', although sometimes, no doubt when feeling annoyed or at odds with life, he would rudely refer to the inoffensive Regardie as 'that worm'. In view of the nomadic life lived by Crowley and his entourage at that time, a life that included being thrown out of hotels and a visit from detectives who believed that a patent coffee-grinder was a machine for the illegal manufacture of heroin, it is surprising how much of the traditional magical lore Regardie managed to acquire during his three hectic years with his teacher.

An occultist who was also associated with Crowley at about the same period has told me that he himself often took four or five days to recover from a week-end with Crowley.

'One had little sleep,' he told me, 'and one seemed to spend twenty-four hours a day, talking, playing chess, drinking brandy, and listening to the recitation of poetry. If, on top of all this, one was also studying Crowley's magical system the strain was almost insupportable.'

Regardie eventually parted from Crowley and, whatever may have been the immediate cause of their break, I suspect that the strain of Crowley's company had become too much for his pupil, in spite of the latter's undoubted intellectual and magical abilities. Nevertheless, I do not think that there can be any doubt that Crowley was a major formative factor in Regardie's intellectual and philosophical development—I feel sure that Regardie's years with Crowley were the most important in his whole life—and nowhere is Crowley's influence more apparent in the writings of Regardie than in *The Tree of Life*, his first book, published by Rider in 1932.

The Tree of Life, in my own opinion the best introduction to practical occultism that has ever been written, was dedicated to 'Marsyas', a name under which Crowley had personalised himself in his poem *Aha*,[1] and included some lengthy quotations from 'Marsyas' himself. It would, however, be a gross mistake to consider *The Tree of Life* as being purely derived from Crowley and his teachings, for it excluded all specifically Thelemite (Crowleyan) elements and, although its author was at the time under the mistaken impression that the Golden Dawn had been defunct for many years, it largely consisted of a restatement of the original pre-1900 G.D. magical system that someone, presumably Mathers, had synthesised from so many diverse elements and sources.

The *Tree of Life* and its companion volume, *The Garden of Pomegranates*, created something of a sensation in the Temples of the Alpha et Omega and the Stella Matutina. It was true, of course, that Crowley had published even more complete versions of the same material over twenty years before, but the volumes of the *Equinox* and 777 had been privately printed in small editions, while Regardie's books, on the other hand, were issued by England's major occult publisher and enjoyed a comparatively wide circulation. The members of the A.O., led by E. J. Langford-Garstin and Mrs. Tranchell-Hayes since the death

---

[1] Marsyas was, in classical mythology, one of the more notable of the Satyrs. Crowley probably chose the name because, in Ancient Rome, the statue of Marsyas was notorious as the site at which many prostitutes plied their trade.

of Mrs. Mathers, seem to have been particularly annoyed; Langford-Garstin actually went to the length of writing to Regardie asking him never again to mention the name of the Golden Dawn in print. Dion Fortune, never averse to disagreeing with her former colleagues, took the opposite point of view and wrote a long article for the *Occult Review* in which she not only praised Regardie's books but gave an enthusiastic welcome to the bound edition of Crowley's *Magick in Theory and Practice*—in a later issue of the same magazine Langford-Garstin replied with a strong defence of the traditional occult secrecy. The Chiefs of the Stella Matutina seem to have been undecided as to what attitude to take; one of them wrote a letter to Dion Fortune saying how much he agreed with her point of view, and, simultaneously, a letter to Langford-Garstin in which he said how irresponsible he considered Dion Fortune to be. Unfortunately the letters were placed in the wrong envelopes and the Stella Matutina failed in its attempt to ingratiate itself with both parties.

In 1934 Regardie joined the Stella Matutina and made a rapid progress through the grades of that organisation. He found the Stella Matutina in a state of demoralisation and decay. Many of the original Knowledge Lectures had been withdrawn or heavily amended, largely because they were beyond the capacities of the Chiefs. These same Chiefs claimed extraordinarily exalted grades, but their claims were belied by their own magical ineptitude and ignorance of that which they purported to teach. To give only one example of this ignorance Regardie found that no one in his Temple knew how to play Enochian chess,[2] the Order chessmen being unmounted, thus making it clear that they had never been actually used. He constructed his own boards and, one by one, challenged his Chiefs to a game—all refused with one excuse or another. Rightly or wrongly Regar-

[2] Enochian chess, in which the chessmen were Egyptian gods and the board one of the Enochian Tablets, was taught in all the early Temples; normally it takes four players to play the game, but one, or even two, of the players can be spirits—W. B. Yeats used to play against Mr. and Mrs. Mathers with a 'spirit' taking the fourth corner of the board. The knowledge of how to play the game seems to have survived in the A.O. and the Cromlech Temple, for some years ago I was taught the game by an initiate of the Bristol Hermanubis Temple.

die came to the conclusion that the Order's teachings would not survive unless they were published; he therefore left the Stella Matutina and deliberately broke the oath of secrecy he had taken at his initiation by publishing the majority of the Golden Dawn manuscripts in four large volumes.

The publication of the first of these volumes, which contained the Knowledge Lectures of the Outer Order, had a shattering effect on both the Stella Matutina and the A.O. and within a year or two both organisations became dormant, for although they carried on a shadowy existence they no longer took neophytes. With their secrets available to all there seemed little point in carrying on. The A.O. took its Temple banners and buried them, together with the personal magical instruments of Mrs. Tranchell-Hayes, Soror Ex Fide Fortis, in a cliff-top garden on the south coast. Thirty years later, in the autumn of 1966, the cliff crumbled away and the box containing these magical impedimenta fell into the sea and was washed up on to a beach, where they were found by some passing visitors. A photograph of them was published in the *Daily Telegraph* along with a statement that 'experts' said that they had belonged to a witch!

Additional Note The late Israel Regardie's impact on modern occultism is, so I understand, to be the subject of a forthcoming study by Mr Gerald Suster.

CHAPTER EIGHTEEN

Dion Fortune and the Fraternity of the Inner Light

After her break with Mrs. Mathers Dion Fortune concentrated her attention on building up her Fraternity of the Inner Light. She gave her followers their preliminary training by means of a series of correspondence courses and they were later initiated into the 'Lesser Mysteries', roughly equivalent to the Outer Order of the Golden Dawn, and eventually passed on into the 'Greater Mysteries', equivalent to the old Inner Order, the R.R. et A.C.

Most of the correspondence course pupils had been originally attracted into the orbit of the Inner Light by Dion Fortune's occult books and articles; most of these were rather vulgar pot-boiling journalism, but one book, *The Mystical Qabalah*, is undoubtedly a classic of the Western Tradition. While the Qabalistic system taught in this book bears little resemblance to the original Judaic Qabalah, it does convey, in a fairly easily comprehensible form, the main outlines of the Golden Dawn's own version of the Christian Qabalah of the fifteenth, sixteenth and seventeenth centuries. Oddly enough, it is marred by one or two strange variations from the Golden Dawn's system,[1] but I do not know whether these were accidental or derived from some private revelation or interpretation of the author.

Dion Fortune was a powerful medium and she practiced a similar type of trance-mediumship to that which was so popular

[1] E.g. Samael, not Sandalphon is stated to be the Angel of Malkuth, the heads of the Serpent are said to have only ascended as far as Tiphareth, while the tradition taught that they rose unto Daath, or Knowledge.

in certain Temples of the Stella Matutina. It must be admitted however, that the intellectual, philosophical and ethical content of the messages received through her is of a far higher standard than the generality of such communications. Some of them, published under the title of the *Cosmic Doctrine*, contain a good deal that is of great interest to students of the Christian Qabalah.

During the early years of its existence the Inner Light used largely unchanged versions of the Golden Dawn initiation rituals, and, as has been stated in a previous chapter, had a semi-amicable relationship with the Stella Matutina. After Regardie had begun to publish his revelations, however, alterations were steadily introduced and eventually the ceremonials used bore no resemblance to those of the Golden Dawn although they were, of course, constructed on the same principles. While I am under no oath of secrecy concerning these rituals I do not wish to reproduce any part of them as one of them, at least, is still being worked. I will merely say that the first of these rituals is based on a quasi-masonic symbolism (there is much concerning the 'rough ashlar' and the 'perfect ashlar') and that certain rather ludicrous information (such as that asbestos and honey-bee were brought to Earth from Venus by a 'Master of the Wisdom') derived from Dion Fortune's mediumship, is conveyed to the candidate.

Dion Fortune died shortly after the second World War and for some years the Inner Light carried on in the tradition that she had established. In the 'fifties and 'sixties there was, however, a marked change of emphasis. First of all came the introduction of practices alien to the Western Tradition derived from the more eccentric fringes of occultism and of physical and psychological therapy; thus members were encouraged to struggle through the monumentally boring writings of Alice A. Bailey, the physical exercises of the Alexander technique, and the weird processes of dianetics and scientology. Later came the abandonment of mediumship and its replacement by something called 'mediation', in which the seer supposedly has mind-to-mind contact with Masters on the 'inner planes'.

I have read many of the A.F. (Aquarian Formula) papers which contain the teachings received through 'mediation', and

I can only say that if the 'Inner Plane Adepti' are responsible for these communications, then these same Adepti are muddled in their thinking, incapable of writing even mediocre English, verbose, sentimental, and possessed of much the same religious outlook as a rather backward Sicilian peasant-woman, A E. Waite writ large, but devoid of Waite's intellectual content. The process of change was completed by abandoning the grade-structure and placing all members in the first degree and, at the same time, abolishing the initiation oath and replacing it with a feeble injunction to use discretion in one's dealings with others. Today the Inner Light can no longer be considered a magical fraternity, it rather more resembles a heterodox semi-Christian cult, rather like the Liberal Catholic Church of the Theosophists.

This abandonment of the magical tradition does not seem to have met with any concerted opposition from the members of the Fraternity, but after a time, some of them 'voted with their feet' and left the organisation. Two groups formed by these ex-members are of some interest. The first, and larger, is centred in Gloucestershire and is closely associated with the Helios Book Service and the Helios Publishing Company. It runs a first-rate correspondence couse on the Qabalah using a book by 'Gareth Knight', the rather romantic pseudonym of a former member of the Inner Light, as its text-book. Some occultists have a very high opinion of this book but, while it has many good points, I feel that it is marred by a rather heavily pietistic attitude and some scientological clap-trap brought over from the post-Dion Fortune Inner Light. The second group is centred in London and, from what little I know of it, seems to be largely working on the lines of research into the Golden Dawn's Enochian system.

Additional Note Readers who are interested in the astral and ceremonial workings of Dion Fortune and her pupils will find much of importance in Mr Alan Richardson's books *Priestess* and *Dancers to the Gods*.

CHAPTER NINETEEN

Later Crowleyan Derivatives

One of the first of Crowley's American native disciples was a young seaman named C. Russell. Russell did not remain long in the navy, however, for, inspired by Crowley's experiments with haschish (described in the early numbers of the *Equinox*), he had decided to use cocaine as a way to expand his consciousness, to 'loosen the girders of the soul'. He had therefore injected himself with some forty grains of this substance—somewhere between five and ten times the normally lethal dose—and attempted various improbable feats, such as setting glass on fire by will-power. The physicians who saved his life decided that the U.S. Navy had no use for magicians, and accordingly he was discharged.

In the early 'twenties he joined Crowley at his Sicilian 'Abbey of Thelema' and here he seems to have had various quarrels with his Master who, after all, was not a particularly easy man to get on with. As the climax to one of these disagreements he ascended a nearby rock, taking an oath neither to come down nor to let water touch his face for a period of eight days.[1]

A day or two later he came down from his eminence, hurled

[1] Mr. Russell is referred to in Symond's *Great Beast* as Frater Genesthai and in Crowley's *Confessions* as Godwin. In general I have not used the real names of any living personalities unless I have had their permission to do so, but in this case the real identity of 'Genesthai' has already been made public in a recent book by Louis T. Culling. In fairness to Mr. Russell it should be stated that he has in preparation his own account of the Sicilian events. This, when published, should make fascinating reading, and will differ considerably from the account given by Crowley and Symonds.

his diary at Crowley, and hurried off into the local town for a shave. The barber was still lathering him, when he suddenly remembered his oath not to let water touch his face, leapt out of his chair, and hurried down the street, soap dripping from his face. He returned only temporarily to the Abbey and then went back, via Australia, to the U.S.A.

In 1931 the following advertisement began to appear in the pages of the American magazine *Occult Digest*:

A short-cut to Initiation
The Choronzon Club,
Box ABC Chicago, Illinois

The Choronzon Club, or, as it was later to call itself, the Great Brotherhood of God, was an independent magical order, led by Russell and teaching an odd variation of the systems used in the Golden Dawn and Crowley's O.T.O.

Now Choronzon, it must be explained, was 'that Mighty Devil' (as he was termed by the sixteenth-century occultist Dee) whom Crowley had evoked to visible appearance some twenty years before, and whom both Mathers and Crowley regarded as the spiritual embodiment of all that is dispersed, deformed, unbalanced and chaotic.[2] Whether or not Russell was in any sense dabbling with Satanism I cannot say, but he certainly turned the Golden Dawn magical system upside down; the Pentagrams which he taught his initiates, for example, were the same as those used in the Golden Dawn but drawn upside down. A pentagram drawn in this way is regarded as evil by most occultists—symbolic of the triumph of matter over Spirit, a sophisticated equivalent of the Lord's Prayer mumbled backwards by an evilly-disposed peasant.[3]

Russell had his own private interpretation of Crowley's new gospel of Thelema, the *Book of the Law*, and claimed that Crowley had failed to carry out his own theory of 'slaying the

[2] Mathers regarded Choronzon as the principle of absolute evil, Crowley, on the other hand, did not believe in the existence of evil as an absolute, only as a relative.

[3] I suspect that Russell would deny this equivalence and have his own involved explanation of his use of these averse pentagrams.

pairs of opposites'. To this he added his own variations of the sexual magic taught by the O.T.O. He abandoned the practice of 'magical masturbation' as taught in the VIII° of the O.T.O., and replaced it with what he called 'Dianism'—the practice usually known as Karezza. Karezza is sexual intercourse without orgasm, often continued for several hours, and strongly disapproved of by most psychologists and sexologists. Russell taught his pupils to continue Karezza until they reached what he called the 'Borderland' state, a sort of hallucinatory trance in which each participant in the sexual act regards the other as a personalisation of his or her own 'Holy Guardian Angel'.[4] After the members of the 'Great Brotherhood of God' had become reasonably proficient in this practice they were taught the IX° sexual magic of the O.T.O. in a comparatively orthodox fashion.

Like most other people, Americans are attracted by short-cuts, and Russell's organisation soon had several Lodges, mostly on the West Coast, each under the direction of an official called the 'Neighbourhood Primate'. Mr. Louis T. Culling, who has recently had published a short book called *The Complete Magick Curriculum of the Secret Order G.˙.B.˙.G.˙.*; was 'Neighbourhood Primate' of the San Diego Lodge, and, according to him, the Order was closed down in 1937. Russell, however—who, after all, should know the truth of the matter—denies this and states that he merely desired to get rid of Culling and, so that this aim might be peacefully achieved, informed him that the G.B.G. was closing down. In any case Mr. Culling continues to operate at least one Lodge using the system devised by Russell in the 'thirties and I believe it probable that Mr. Russell himself continues to run some sort of magical or neo-Gnostic organisation. I am sure, however, that the teachings and the techniques of the latter body have undergone a considerable development during the last thirty years.

There was some revival of interest in Crowley during the

---

[4] Another extraordinary thing done by Russell was to make his neophytes take an oath to 'regard any event as a particular dealing between myself and my Holy Guardian Angel'—an oath that is normally regarded as that pertaining to the exalted grade of Magister Templi.

late 'thirties and 'forties, and Crowley began to gather an American following of greater orthodoxy than Russell, mostly in California. The leader of this Californian group, whom I shall call Frater 156, was a pleasant man of capable magical ability, but, after a time, personal quarrels began to arise between him and other members of the Lodge. Crowley did not wish to offend this man, for whom he had a considerable admiration, but, on the other hand, he did wish to remove him from his position as Chief of the Lodge. With tongue in cheek he devised the perfect method of doing this; it was time, he said, that Frater 156's great abilities were recognised, he must become a god! As such, of course, he would have to cease engaging himself in such petty mundane things as running the Californian Lodge of the O.T.O.—after his apotheosis he would simply be consulted for advice on the sort of major problems that concern the gods. Frater 156 was enthusiastic; he performed the magical retirement and long series of rituals prescribed by his Master, duly became, or thought he became, a god, and handed over his Chieftainship to Jack Parsons, a brilliant American physical chemist who had been largely responsible for the foundation of the now famous Cal. Tech. and had been a follower of Crowley since 1939.

Parsons managed his Lodge admirably, and it was not until 1945 that he became involved in any major difficulty. In that year he met L. Ron Hubbard, future founder of the strange scientific cults of dianetics and scientology, and struck up a close and immediate friendship with him; in a letter to Crowley, written at the beginning of 1946, Parsons said of Hubbard:

> He is a gentleman, red hair, green eyes, honest and intelligent and we have become great friends. Although he has no formal training in magic he has an extraordinary amount of experience and understanding in the field. Ron appears to have some sort of highly developed astral vision. He describes his angel as a beautiful winged woman with red hair whom he calls the Empress and who has guided him through his life and saved him many times.

During the first World War Crowley had written a novel called the *Butterfly Net*, later to be published under the name of *Moonchild*. This novel tells the story of a magical operation based on the theory that a particular type of spirit can be induced to incarnate in an unborn human embryo[5] by surrounding the mother with the appropriate influences, carrying out certain rituals, etc. Parsons wished to carry out such an operation designed to achieve the incarnation of Babalon—an aspect of the great Mother-goddess Nuit—in an unborn child, and he decided that Hubbard would make an ideal co-worker.

In order to obtain a woman prepared to bear this magical child Parsons and Hubbard engaged themselves for eleven days in rituals. These do not seem to have produced any marked result until January 14th when, so Parsons said, Hubbard had a candle knocked out of his hand. Parsons went on to record that Hubbard called him 'and we observed a brownish-yellow light about seven feet high. I brandished a magical sword and it disappeared. Ron's right arm was paralysed for the rest of the night.'

On the following night, so Parsons said, Hubbard had a vision of an enemy of the O.T.O. and 'attacked the figure and pinned it to the door with four throwing knives with which he is an expert.'

All this work seemed to achieve its desired result and, on January 18th, Parsons found a girl who was prepared to become the mother of Babalon, and to go through the required incarnation rituals. During these rituals, which took place on the first three days of March 1946, Parsons was High Priest and had sexual intercourse with the girl, while Hubbard who was present acted as skryer, seer, or clairvoyant and described what was supposed to be happening on the astral plane.

Parsons believed that he had been successful in this operation and wrote to Crowley:

I can hardly tell you or decide how much to write. I am under the command of extreme secrecy. I have had the most

[5] Crowley believed that the human soul does not incarnate into an unborn child until about the end of the third month of pregnancy.

important devastating experience of my life.

To which Crowley, for once at a loss to know what was going on, replied:

> You have me completely puzzled by your remarks. I thought I had the most morbid imagination but it seems I have not. I cannot form the slightest idea what you can possibly mean.

The same day Crowley wrote to Karl Germer, his heir-apparent to the Headship of the O.T.O.:

> Apparently Parsons or Hubbard or somebody is producing a Moonchild. I get fairly frantic when I contemplate the idiocy of those louts.

Meanwhile Parsons and Hubbard had sealed their friendship by opening a joint bank account—Parsons contributed his life savings of about $17000 while Hubbard put up approximately $1000. This aroused Crowley's suspicions and he wrote to Karl Germer:

> It seems to me on the information of our brethren in California that Parsons has got an illumination in which he has lost all his personal independence. From our brother's account he has given away both his girl[6] and his money. Apparently it is the ordinary confidence trick.

By this time Hubbard had withdrawn some $10,000 from the joint bank account and used it to buy a yacht. The disillusioned Parsons pursued him to Florida, from where he wrote to Crowley on July 5th, 1946:

> Here I am in Miami pursuing the children of my folly. I have them well tied up. They cannot move without going to jail. However, I am afraid that most of the money has

[6] 'Betty', Parsons' girl friend (not to be confused with the would-be mother of Babalon) had by this time transferred her affections to Hubbard.

already been spent. I will be lucky to salvage 3,000 to 5,000 dollars.

According to Parsons Hubbard attempted to escape him 'by sailing at 5.0 p.m. and (I) performed a full invocation to Bartzabel[7] within the Circle at 8.0 p.m. (a curse). At the same time, however, his ship was struck by a sudden squall off the coast which ripped off his sails and forced him back to port where I took the boat in custody.'

Thus ends the strange story of L. Ron Hubbard's connection with the O.T.O.; Parsons himself went on to take the Oath of Antichrist in 1948—at the same time he changed his name to 'Belarion Armiluss Al Dajjal Antichrist'. He died in 1952 when there was an explosion of rocket-fuel in his Laboratory at Pasadena.

In fairness to Mr. Hubbard and his fellow-scientologists it must be said that he has his own explanation of the curious events of 1946. He states that 'certain agencies'—and I assume he means the F.B.I., for they certainly investigated Parsons' Temple—objected to the fact that many nuclear physicists were living under the same roof as Parsons and the 'savage bestial rites' of the O.T.O., and that he, at that time an officer in the U.S. navy, was sent to 'handle the situation'. Hubbard claims that he was completely successful in his mission for 'the black magic group was dispersed and destroyed and has never recovered'.

On the death of Crowley in 1947 the Headship of the O.T.O. passed to Karl Germer, originally one of the German minority of the O.T.O. who had followed Crowley, but now an American.

German devoted a good deal of attention to getting the unpublished works of Crowley into print, and he was responsible for both the first publication of *Magick Without Tears* and the *Book of Wisdom or Folly*, and for the appearance of revised and enlarged versions of the *Vision and the Voice*, the *Book of Lies*, and *777*.

Germer had an interesting relationship with Mr. Kenneth

---

[7] The spirit of Mars.

Grant,[8] a young English disciple of Crowley, whom he chartered in 1951 or 1952 to work the first three grades of the O.T.O. All seems to have gone well for a time, but in 1955 Mr. Grant set up what he called 'New Isis Lodge O.T.O.' working eleven rituals (O° to IX° and a group ritual for Lodge-work) drawn up by himself. At the same time he issued a manifesto which, while I sometimes find it difficult to follow, seems to announce the discovery of a trans-Plutonian planet called Isis (needless to say, this planet, like the 'hypotheticals' of the German Hamburg School of astrology, is completely unknown to exoteric science), and to hint darkly at a new revelation concerning the first chapter of Crowley's *Book of the Law*. A copy of this manifesto was sent to Karl Germer, along with a letter explaining that, for the preservation of secrecy, it was not possible for him to see copies of the new rituals. Germer's response was extremely quick and, on July 20th, 1955, he sent a registered letter to Mr. Grant expelling him from the O.T.O. and withdrawing all authority for the latter to work a 'Camp, Lodge, or Temple of the O.T.O.'.

Germer died in the early 'sixties and was succeeded by a Swiss named Herr Metzger who had been elected to the Headship by the majority of the recognised O.T.O. membership. Herr Metzger is also the patriarch of Crowley's 'Gnostic Catholic Church', whose services are advertised in the Zurich newspapers alongside the announcements of more conventional religious bodies. I have heard that the Swiss version of the 'Gnostic Catholic Mass' is of the utmost respectability, both Priest and Priestess remaining fully clothed throughout the ceremony.

One other small, but interesting, Crowleyan offshoot remains to be mentioned, 'The Fellowship of Ma-Ion'. This group consists of followers of Charles Stansfeld Jones (Frater Achad), the man whom Crowley believed to have discovered the qabalistic key to the *Book of the Law*. After he had allegedly discovered

---

[8] I have given his real name because (a) it is stated in No. 3 of *Man, Myth and Magic* that he was initiated into 'Crowley's occult society' and (b) on the inside dust-cover of Crowley's *Confessions* (which Mr. Grant edited in collaboration with John Symonds) it is stated that he is now Head of the O.T.O. and I presume that this statement was made with his approval.

the numerical key Jones came to the conclusion that the qabalistic correspondences between the Paths of the Tree of Life,
the Tarot trumps etc. taught by the Golden Dawn[9] were quite
incorrect. He therefore introduced many changes; for example
the Hebrew letter Aleph (corresponding to the Tarot card the
Fool), which had been attributed by the Golden Dawn to the
path connecting the Sephiroth Kether and Chokmah, was
attributed by Jones to the thirty-second path connecting Yesod
and Malkuth.

He went on to have a vision which convinced him that the
actual physical shape of the traditional Tree of Life was the
key to the physical structure of the Universe. He described
this vision as follows:

> On April 14th, 1923 e.v. having just completed the m.s.
> of my treatise on the 'Egyptian Revival' or the Ever-Coming
> Son, in which my endeavour was to show that the 'Restored
> Order' of the Paths of the Qabalistic Tree of Life was likely
> to be the correct one, since it indicated the Universal Tradi-
> tion as symbolised by the Keys of Hermes, I was rewarded
> by the opening up of an amazing further possibility in
> regard to the design of the 'Tree of Life' itself.
>
> It was between 8.30 and 9.30 p.m. on the above date,
> that the 'Tree' began to GROW, and proved itself, to my mind,
> to be the veritable anatomy of Ra-Hoor-Khuit, Evercoming
> between the two Infinities.

After this he developed his own interpretation of the Book
of the Law,[10] came to believe in a coming 'Ma-Ion era of Truth
and Justice', and, strangely enough, managed to combine these
beliefs with membership of the Catholic Church.

The 'Fellowship of Ma-Ion' has a few members in the United
States and Canada.

---

[9] Many of these correspondences are given in R. G. Torrens' *The Golden
Dawn—its Inner Teachings* (Neville Spearman, 1970).

[10] So many of Crowley's pupils came to the conclusion that Crowley had
misinterpreted the *Book of the Law* that one would be inclined to agree
with them, were it not for the fact that their own interpretations all clash
so violently with one another!

CHAPTER TWENTY

An Alchemical Rebirth of the Golden Dawn

In the middle 'twenties three initiates of the Stella Matutina's Hermes Temple, situated in Bristol, resigned from it as they no longer felt themselves in agreement with the markedly Anthroposophical tone of the teachings given out by the Chiefs of that Temple. These three initiates, all full Adepti Minores,[1] did not, however, completely abandon the practice of magic but instead worked together as a small informal group, largely specialising in a study of the alchemical tradition and almost completely abandoning the astral travel techniques and the semi-spiritualist practices of the Stella Matutina.

In 1939 they joined forces with two Anglican clergymen, both of whom had formerly been high-ranking members of the Cromlech Temple and the Alpha et Omega, but had, some years before, withdrawn into inactivity after there had been an episcopal enquiry into the occult activities of a small group of clergymen in East Anglia—all members of the Cromlech Temple.

At this time Regardie had already published his *My Rosicrucian Adventure* and was half-way through publishing his four-volume edition of the rites and lectures of the Golden Dawn. While the five Adepti did not agree with Regardie's action in breaking the oath of secrecy which he had taken

---

[1] Nominally one of them was an Exempt Adept and another a Magister Templi—but the high-grades of the Stella Matutina were largely meaningless.

upon his initiation, they felt, to some extent at least, sympathetic to the motives which had led him to do so. They were sure that the Golden Dawn synthesis was worthy of preservation, that at least one Temple must survive in which the original system was taught in its entirety. To this end they established the Hermanubis Temple in Bristol, working only the grades of the original Golden Dawn and strongly discouraging the astral adventuring that had been so popular in both Florence Farr's 'The Sphere' and in the later Stella Matutina.

The five deliberately selected the name Hermanubis for their Temple, for they wished to emhasise their links with the original Order, and therefore chose to revive the name of a Temple (probably German) that had become defunct fifty years earlier.[2] In view of Regardie's publication of the initiation rituals of the Stella Matutina the new Chiefs made some changes in these 'so that the Temple members might develop a group-mind of their own,'[3] but these were of a very minor nature.

The Chiefs of Hermanubis were also much more selective in their choice of neophytes than were the Chiefs of the original Golden Dawn and Stella Matutina Temples; by 1949 there were still only fourteen members of the new Temple.

The Hermanubis Temple was also responsible for a revival of the study of the western alchemical tradition. In the original Golden Dawn there had been a small group that had practiced alchemy under the guidance of the Rev. W. A. Ayton, but this type of work seems to have fallen into abeyance shortly after 1900; it is significant that when Regardie came to compile his *Golden Dawn* he was completely unable to trace any operation based on the alchemical section of the G.D. manuscript known as Z2. The Bristol occultists, however, have carried out numerous alchemical workings based on Z2;[4] in view of Regardie's failure to trace a working of this type I feel that

[2] See Appendix G.
[3] I have never been able to completely understand the average occultist's passion for secrecy and belief that a rite becomes ineffectual if it is published; after all the Canon of the Mass has been printed in literally millions of copies, but, nonetheless, it remains an extremely effective ceremony.
[4] They have also revived the art of full ceremonial divination, another neglected aspect of Z2.

it is well worth while to give the following condensed extracts from the record of a Z2 alchemical operation carried out in Bristol some years ago (there are some odd changes of tense in this record, I have felt it best to leave these unamended):

The Temple is arranged as in the 0°=0° Grade of the G.D. in the Outer.

The Alchemist announces 'Hekas Hekas Este Bebeloi', then takes the Sword and carries out the Lesser Banishing Rituals of the Pentagram and Hexagram therewith.

Returning to the Cubical Altar of the Universe the Alchemist takes up the Fire Wand and goes to the Fire Quarter. Circumambulating deosil he recites from the Chaldean Oracles of Zoroaster: 'And when, after all the phantoms have vanished, thou shalt see that Holy and Formless Fire, that Fire which darts and flashes through the hidden depths of the Universe, hear thou the Voice of Fire.'

On returning to the South the Alchemist traces the Fire Pentagram with the Kerub of Fire in its centre, saying 'OIP TEAA PDOCE.[5] By the letters of the Fourth Watch Tower I invoke the Angels of the Great Southern Quadrangle of Fire.

Returning to the Altar of the Double Cube the Alchemist replaces Fire Wand and takes up the Cup which he then carries to the appropriate quarter for the first sprinkling. The Alchemist then again does deosil reciting from Zoroaster: 'So therefore the Priest who governeth the works of Fire must sprinkle with the lustral water of the loud resounding sea.' On returning to the West the Alchemist carries out the second sprinkling and makes the Water Pentagram with the Sigil of Scorpio in its midst saying 'MPH ARSL GAIOL. By the letters of the Second Watchtower I invoke the Angels of the Great Western Quadrangle of Water.'

Returning to the Altar as before the Alchemist replaces the Cup and takes up the Dagger of Air which he takes to the East from where, after striking the air, he goes deosil reciting from Zoroaster: 'Such a Fire existeth, extending through the rushings of the Air. And even a Fire formless

---

[5] These strange words are in the so-called Angelic or Enochian language.

whence cometh the image of a voice. And even a flashing Light, abounding, revolving, whirling forth, crying aloud.' On returning to the East the Alchemist makes the Air Pentagram with the Sigil of Kerubic Air in its midst saying: 'ORO IBAH AOZPI. By the letters of the First Watchtower I invoke the Angels of the Great Eastern Quadrangle of Air.'

The Alchemist replaces the Dagger upon the Altar and takes up the Disc which he takes to the North for the ritual shaking after which he again goes deosil reciting 'Stoop not down into the darkly splendid work wherein continually lieth a faithless depth and Hedes wrapped in gloom, delighting in unintelligible images, precipitous, winding; a black ever-rolling abyss ever espousing a body unluminous, formless and void.' On returning to the North the Alchemist makes Earth Pentagram with Kerubic Earth symbol in its midst saying 'MOR DIAL HCTGA. By the letters of the Third Watchtower I invoke the Angels of the Great Northern Quadrangle of Earth.'

The Alchemist takes up the burning Incense of Abramelin and turning to the Banner of the East invokes the Spirit by Pentagram crying aloud 'EXARP BITOM NANTA HCOMA. By the letters of the Tablet of Union I invoke the force of the Spirit of Life.'

The Alchemist replaces the incense and makes the sign of the Rending of the Veil, afterwards saying 'I invoke the Guardians of the Universe and the Guardians of the Order to be likewise the Guardians of this Oratory and this my Scin-Laeca. Guard and inspire me so that the Yechidah may shine through my magical mirror of the universe so that I may become partaker in the Life and Secrets of the Light Eternal.'

The Alchemist goes three times deosil and then faces last, crying:

'Holy art Thou Lord of the Universe!

Holy art Thou Whom Nature hath not Formed!

Holy art Thou, the Vast and Mighty One!

Lord of Light and Darkness!'

The Alchemist then places the material basis in a flask and after the Invocation of a blind Jupiterian[6] force leaves it, sealed, in a gentle heat for three days. At the end of this period he evokes a Jupiterian spirit and then fastens a Liebeg condenser to the flask. After distillation he grinds the solid left in the flask to a powder, replaces it in its original container and pours on to it the distilled fluid. He then reseals the flask.

The Alchemist places the flask upon a Flashing Tablet of Jupiter and, standing at the East of the Altar, places his left hand upon it. Holding his Lotus Wand, by the Aries band, in his right hand the Alchemist conjures the general forces of Chesed[7] to act within the flask, making the required signs and sigils with the Wand. When finished he raises the flask in the air with both hands saying 'Arise herein to action, Ye Forces of Light Divine'.

The Alchemist now lets the sealed flask remain at a gentle heat in a water bath until the material basis turns completely black,[8] and, when this has been achieved, he places the flask upon the North of the Altar and invokes Saturn. Then he takes his Lotus Wand by the black band and says: 'The Voice of the Alchemist said unto me, let me enter the Path of Darkness, for thus may I achieve the Realm of Light'.

The Alchemist then again gently distils the material basis and, once again, returns the liquid to the solid, re-sealing the flask and placing it in a water bath until all is re-dissolved. The Alchemist then takes the flask to the West of the Altar and invokes Cauda Draconis[9] and the waning Moon. He places the flask upon a Flashing Tablet of Luna and places it

---

[6] The ultimate aim of this operation was the production of a healing compound and such compounds are generally classified under Jupiter.

[7] The Sephirah on the Qabalistic Tree of Life to which Jupiter is attributed.

[8] From the *Book of Results* it is clear that the material did not, in fact, turn black. The alchemist decided that this was because its nature was not so to do and, after evoking a Saturnian elemental whose task was to examine the astral appearance of the material, he decided that it was astrally black and proceeded to the next stage of the operation.

[9] Cauda Draconis, 'the tail of the Dragon', is the south node of the Moon.

exposed to the moonlight for nine nights, the first night being that of the full Moon. The material basis is then distilled and redissolved as before.

The Alchemist then takes the flask to the East of the Altar and invokes the waxing Moon and Caput Draconis, then he replaces the flask on the Tablet of Luna and leaves it exposed to the moonlight for nine nights, this time the last night being that of the full moon. Again the material basis is distilled and re-dissolved.

The Alchemist takes the flask to the South of the Altar and invokes the forces of Tiphareth and Sol after which, the Sun being in Leo, the flask is exposed to the Sun for six days from 8.30 a.m. to 8.30 p.m. while standing upon the appropriate Flashing Tablet. Afterwards the flask is stood again upon the Altar and the Alchemist says 'Child of Earth, long hast thou dwelt in Darkness, quit the Night and seek the Day'. He then takes the Lotus Wand by the white band, making the correct signs and sigils and says 'I formulate in thee the Invoked Forces of Light' reciting the Words of Power from the Great Enochian Watchtowers.

The Alchemist now evokes an elemental from the material and checks by the nature of its colouring whether the material basis has reached the correct condition; if it has not done so he repeats the lunar and solar workings.

The Alchemist now holds the Lotus Wand over the flask and draws the Qabalistic Flaming Sword so that its point descends into the material basis, after this he stands the flask on the East of the Altar and invokes Mars. When the invocation is successfully completed the flask is placed between the Black and White Pillars of the Temple of the G.D. in the Outer and remains there for five days upon a Flashing Tablet of Mars.

The Alchemist then again distils, but this time does not re-dissolve the solid which is, for the moment, kept separate. The fluid is taken and into it is invoked the forces of Mercury after which it is placed upon a Flashing Tablet and exposed to the Sun for eight days. The solid is ground up into a powder and into it is invoked the forces of Jupiter, after which it is left in the darkness upon the Flashing Tablet for four days.

Upon the Altar of the Double Cube the Alchemist places Flashing Tablets of Earth, Air, Fire, and Water together with the Pantacle of Earth, the Wand of Fire, the Cup of Water, and the Dagger of Air.[10] He then carries out the Greater Ritual of the Pentagram, firstly invoking Fire with the Wand to act upon the powder, secondly invoking Water with the Cup to act upon the liquid, thirdly invoking active and passive Spirit with the White Band of the Lotus Wand to act upon both the powder and the liquid, fourthly invoking Air, with the Dagger to act upon the liquid, and fifthly invoking Earth with the pantacle to act upon the powder. The vessels are now left upon the Altar for five days.

The Alchemist then leaves the vessels untouched but removes the Elemental Tablets, replacing them with a white and gold Tablet of Kether, he identifies himself with his own Holy Guardian Angel and invokes Kether.

The powder and the liquid are now again joined together and exposed to the rays of the Sun for ten days. The flask is then replaced upon the Altar, standing upon a Flashing Tablet of Venus, and the Alchemist invokes the forces of Venus. He then leaves the flask for seven days upon the Tablet at the end of which period he places it in a water-bath for a similar length of time.

The Alchemist again distils, the liquid being placed aside to serve as a medicine.[11] The powder is placed by the Alchemist in a crucible and heated to white heat and allowed to slowly cool seven times, on seven consecutive days.

Here ends my condensation of this extraordinary operation. It only remains to add that according to the 'Book of Results' the end product was 'like unto a glittering powder' and that its use produced 'many strange and wonderful results'.

In 1959 the Chiefs of Hermanubis chartered a London

[10] These are the 'Four Elemental Magical Weapons' of the Golden Dawn.
[11] If the *Book of Results* is to be believed its effects were remarkable when it was taken, in minute doses, for medicinal purposes.

Daughter-Temple which revived the name of Isis Urania, no doubt to reaffirm its fidelity to the original Golden Dawn tradition. Only the five grades of the Outer Order are worked in London, there being no separate 'Vault of the Adepti'. Those London members who are sufficiently advanced are attached to the Bristol 'Vault'; there are few of these, however, for the Chiefs of the London Temple seem to be quite as selective in their choice of neophytes as do their colleagues in the Mother-temple.

Additional Note I am now satisfied that the modern Bristol Temple mentioned in this chapter had no connection with either the original Golden Dawn or the Cromlech Temple.

CHAPTER TWENTY-ONE

The Contemporary Witch–Cult

There are a substantial number of people in England who are practicing, or believe that they are practicing, traditional witchcraft, which they suppose to be the still-surviving fertility-religion of prehistoric Europe. One of the more publicity-conscious of these cultists, who calls himself 'King of the Witches', claims to have no less than 107 groups, known as covens, each with thirteen members, under his control. This very large figure must be treated with a good deal of scepticism; nonetheless, from personal knowledge I believe that there are somewhere between one and two thousand individuals who are sufficiently interested in the subject to be active members of covens, and, no doubt, there are many other people on the fringe of these organised activities.

Those non-members of the cult who have examined the phenomenon of twentieth-century witchcraft are generally of the opinion that the whole movement is no more than twenty years old, the creation of a retired Malayan customs official named Gerald Brousseau Gardner. I have strong reason to believe that their conclusion is incorrect.

In 1953 a former tutor of mine introduced me to Louis Umfraville Wilkinson, then living in the small Dorset village of Hazelbury Bryant. Wilkinson, the son of the proprietor-headmaster of a preparatory school in Sussex, had lived an interesting and full life.

He had originally gone to Oxford but, on being sent down

for blasphemy, had transferred himself to Cambridge, where he had become friendly with the Powys brothers—he is the 'Archangel' of John Cowper Powys' autobiography—and in their company he had the, by no means unique, satisfaction of deeply offending Frederick Rolfe, 'Baron Corvo', author of *Hadrian* VII, then living in Venice.

Subsequently he had written excellent but seldom-read novels under the name of Louis Marlow, had contributed reviews to Vol. III No. 1 of Crowley's *Equinox*, and had lectured widely on English literature. In 1947 he had infuriated a Brighton local paper by reading the beautiful *Last Ritual*, Aleister Crowley's funeral service, at the municipal crematorium—one national newspaper described it as a 'Black Mass'.

We talked for a while of Oscar Wilde—Wilkinson had been the precocious Radley schoolboy who had corresponded with him during his imprisonment—and of Crowley, whose joint literary executor he was. He showed me Crowley's amusingly annotated, vellum bound, volumes of Swinburne, and read me 'Dolores' in his clear and beautiful voice. Then, in casual conversation, much-interrupted by the intrusion of his wife's elegant cats, he said that Crowley had told him that, as a young man, he had been offered initiation into the witch-cult, but had refused it as he 'didn't want to be bossed around by women'.[1]

I was intrigued; like many other people I had read the anthropological fantasies of Margaret Murray with mingled interest, amusement, and scepticism, but I had no idea that there were alleged witch-covens surviving into the twentieth century.

I politely asked him if he considered it possible that Crowley had been indulging in a gentle leg-pull, to which he replied that, while Crowley was apt to indulge in such jokes, in this case he was telling the truth; for, in the late 'thirties or early 'forties, he had himself become friendly with members of a witch-coven operating in the New Forest.

The social composition of this group, he told me, was a

[1] I have since heard from two independent sources that Crowley had made this claim to them.

peculiar amalgam of middle-class intellectuals with the local peasantry, and, while the foundation of the group might have dated from after the 1921 publication of Margaret Murray's *Witch Cult in Western Europe*, he was himself reasonably confident that there had been a fusion of an authentic surviving folk-tradition with a more intellectual middle-class occultism.

Louis Wilkinson went on to tell me various interesting details of the practices of these Hampshire witches—details which, I felt sure, made it certain that the group was not simply derived from the jaded tastes of middle-class intellectuals who adhered to the theories of Margaret Murray. To give one example, the *Witch Cult in Western Europe* gives two recipes for the 'witches' ointment', both compounds of oil and poisonous herbs, which the book's author considered were probably intended to give pleasant hallucinations of riding on broomsticks, attendance at the Sabbat, etc. The New Forest coven, on the other hand, also used an ointment, but it was simply a heavy grease, largely consisting of bears' fat, rather similar to that used by channel-swimmers and having a similar purpose, for it was simply designed to protect their naked bodies from cold at open-air gatherings. They also used an hallucinogen, but this was fly-agaric, a common British fungi, which they took orally in extremely small doses. Fly-agaric and similar fungi have been used all over the world from time immemorial. It was used by the Vikings when they wished to go berserk and, at the other end of the Euro-Asian land mass, by Siberian shamans to achieve trance. Curiously enough, it seems to have escaped the attention of the hippies in their enthusiastic pursuit of psychedelic experience—probably fortunately for them, for the essential alkaloid is extremely toxic, samples of the fungus vary widely in their potency, and the unwary user can very easily wind up on a mortuary slab.

On at least one occasion the Hampshire witches indulged in human sacrifice—but done in such a way that there could not possibly be any legal unpleasantnesses. This was done in May 1940, when Hitler's invasion was felt to be imminent. The witches felt that it was essential that he should be deterred from invasion plans by a powerful ritual, the central point of which was to be the death of a (volunteer) sacrificial victim. The oldest and frailest member volunteered for sacrifice and left off his protective grease so that he might die of the effects of exposure. Unfortunately enough, it was the coldest May night for many years, and not only the volunteer but two other members of the coven died from pneumonia within the next fortnight.

Unquestionably, however, it was the writings of Gerald Gardner that were responsible for the mushroom-growth of the witch-cult in the 'fifties and 'sixties.

He had been born in June, 1884 and, until his retirement from the Malayan customs service in 1936, had spent much of his life in the Far East. He seems to have dabbled a good deal in the messier fringes of occultism, for he frequented spiritualist mediums, displayed a marked interest in the animistic beliefs of the more primitive Malay peoples, and was a friend of J. S. M. Ward, a bogus Bishop who had at one time been an important official of the Federation of British Industries, who had written some quite good but far-fetched books on masonry, and who ran a peculiar religious-cum-occult community called the Abbey of Christ the King, at first near St. Albans in England and later in Cyprus, where Gardner met him.

In 1940 Gardner joined an allegedly Rosicrucian organisation headed by a daughter of Annie Besant and having its activities centred on the town of Christchurch in Hampshire, where it ran a so-called 'Rosicrucian Theatre'. Here he met, or claimed to have met, members of the witch-cult who were using the 'Rosicrucian' organisation as a casting-net to gather in new recruits for their coven—which was, I suspect, the same coven that Louis Wilkinson had come into contact with. Gardner was eventually initiated into this group and, although he claimed to have been appointed as their publicity officer, he does not seem to have found their simple ceremonies to his liking and he consequently decided to found a more elaborate and romanticised witch-cult of his own.

He had known Aleister Crowley for some time, for he was not only a VII° initiate of the O.T.O. but actually held a Charter authorising him to operate some sort of O.T.O. Lodge

—although, in fact, he never seems to have done this. He accordingly hired Crowley, at a generous fee, to write elaborate rituals for the new 'Gardnerian' witch-cult and, at about the same time, either forged, or procured to be forged, the so-called *Book of Shadows*, allegedly a sixteenth-century witches rule-book, but betraying its modern origins in every line of its unsatisfactory pastiche of Elizabethan English.

In the late 'forties Gardner wrote, under the pseudonym of Scire, a long and almost unreadable novel called *High Magic's Aid*[2] which dealt with magic and witchcraft in mediaeval England. The book seems to have been a resounding flop—five years later I saw the publisher's shelves still groaning under the weight of unsold copies—but it did arouse a little interest among those inclined to such subjects, and Gardner soon acquired a few followers.

In 1954 Rider published Gardner's *Witchcraft Today*—not at all a bad book, for the reader responsible for its acceptance, himself an occult scholar of distinction, managed to blue-pencil most of the more rubbishy passages. The book had some small commercial success and was quite widely reviewed and, as a result of this, new covens, deriving their rituals and teaching more or less from Gardner, began to spring up all over the country.

Unfortunately, Gardner was a sado-masochist with both a taste for flagellation and marked voyeuristic tendencies. Heavy scourging was therefore incorporated into most of his rituals and what Gardner called the 'Great Rite' was sexual intercourse between the High Priest and the High Priestess while surrounded by the rest of the coven.[3]

By 1964, when Gardner died, there were many covens ultimately deriving from him, but some of which had abandoned

[2] While the book appeared under the imprint of Michael Houghton Ltd., an occult bookseller of Museum Street in London, I believe that Gardner himself met the costs of production.

[3] It is, of course, true that public sexual intercourse played an important role in the magico-religious rites of many primitive and some civilised communities (e.g. Sparta). In addition, such sexual activity has been used by certain advanced occultists under carefully controlled conditions; I am satisfied, however, that Gardner introduced his 'Great Rite' for no other purpose than to satisfy his own personal tastes.

the more extreme flagello-sexual excesses.

Today the witch-cult is split into five or six competing sections, some of them still with a marked bias towards sexuality —one of these has an extraordinary 'death-spell' which involves the Priest and Priestess indulging in the no doubt very uncomfortable process of having intercourse through the hole drilled through the middle of an allegedly neolithic stone relic!

Other contemporary covens are much less permissive in their attitudes towards sex and largely engage themselves in healing work achieved by means of a combination of charms and herbal remedies.

Probably the most interesting aspects of contemporary witchcraft are the one or two surviving pre-Gardnerian covens on the one hand and the so-called 'robed covens' on the other. The latter, as their name implies, eschew nudity and combine their worship of the horned-god and the moon-goddess with a certain amount of more orthodox ritual magic, dowsing, astrology, etc.

Additional Note Contemporary Witchcraft continues to be influenced by the more intellectual aspects of the magical tradition. This influence is very apparent in, for example, the intensely readable books of Stewart and Janet Farrar. At least one present day group is practising Enochian magic.

CHAPTER TWENTY-TWO

A New System of Magic

During, or very shortly after, the second World War a friend of mine, then an art-student, now a Chartered Accountant, became friendly with an elderly painter named A. O. Spare. Some forty years earlier Spare had been a most successful artist, for at a very youthful age he had been 'discovered' and enjoyed a good reputation among the art critics of the time. When my friend met him, however, he had been largely forgotten and was living in poverty in an extremely depressing basement flat—damp ran down the walls, the air was filled with a musty odour, vaguely suggestive of both mice and dry rot, and there was a continuous and almost overpowering background of noise, not only from the London 'buses that ran a few feet away, but from the water and drainage pipes that ran, no doubt in defiance of the sanitary regulations, between the ceiling of the basement and the floorboards of the rooms above.

Spare got on quite well with my friend, for they shared a dislike of the artistic fashions of the 'thirties, but they had a violent disagreement on the subjects of spiritualism and magic. Spare had two quite different artistic styles; the first was uniquely his own, the second bore a marked resemblance to the later drawings of William Blake, by whom Spare alleged that he was at times literally possessed. My friend was unimpressed by these claims and talked, in the confident way of youth, of disassociated complexes, schizoid personalities, and the rest of the psychiatric jargon that has now become so drearily familiar. Spare became annoyed and announced that he not only completely believed in magic, but had practiced it for many years and had, in fact, invented a completely new system of practical occultism. This new system, said Spare, was called Zoz or Zos, and he promised my friend to prepare a practical demonstration of it for their next meeting.

The following week my friend arrived at Spare's flat for the demonstration; he had done a little reading during the intervening period and was feeling slightly nervous, nevertheless, he felt that his own firm adherence to the linguistic philosophy of A. J. Ayer would save him from being gobbled up by the demon Asmodeus or, indeed, any other unpleasantnesses.

My friend was surprised to find no magic circle, no burning incense, and no trace of the usual magical apparatus. Instead the table was covered with drawings, many of them consisting of interlocked letters, and Spare, far from being engaged in some ascetic preparation for his working, was eating a slice of pie. The pie being finished, Spare proceeded with his experiment which, he told my friend, was designed to reproduce a phenomenon, common enough in nineteenth-century spiritualism but rare in the twentieth century, known as the apport— he was going to produce living and freshly-cut roses from the atmosphere. At first Spare did not chant or in any way speak. He simply waved a drawing in the air for a minute or two and then replaced it on the table, following this by raising his arms and enunciating, his face contorted with some internal struggle, the word 'Roses'. For a moment there was a tense silence, then, with a crackling, splintering noise, the plaster fell from the ceiling, and a hundred and fifty gallons of mingled sewage and bath water poured over the two from the overhead drainage pipe that had finally exploded under the pressure of a weeks-old blockage.

In spite of this ludicrous adventure there are many points of interest in the new magical system evolved by Spare. Like all magicians he believed that any desire deeply felt in the inmost centre of human consciousness was capable of fulfillment,[1] but he devised new techniques, altogether simpler than

[1] Compare Crowley's doctrine of the 'True Will' (it is interesting to note that Spare was a member of Crowley's A.A. *circa* 1910) and the 'It' (from which Freud derived his concept of the Id) of the unorthodox psychologist Groddeck.

those of the magical tradition, for attaining this fulfillment of desire.[2] There are several of these methods but Spare regarded the construction of what he called 'alphabetic sigils' as the most important of these. To manufacture an alphabetic sigil a sentence, as brief and to the point as possible, is written to express the inner desire. Then some letters are crossed out so that no letter is repeated, and the remaining letters are combined, rather in the fashion of a monogram, to form a sigil. This sigil is then stared at by the magician who lets it sink into his subconscious, and then forgets, as far as he possibly can, the original desire, leaving at 'It' to work, undisturbed, towards its fulfillment.

Spare also believed that spiritual, mental or even physical exhaustion could be used to create magical effects by the utilisation of certain mental exercises intended to draw the desired reality into the vacuum created by the exhaustion. An extension of this was to use a tremendous disappointment, a cessation of belief in some faith, religion, philosophy or even person, to absorb the sum total of the powers originally enshrined in that belief.

It would be premature as yet to decide whether or not Spare's new techniques are sufficiently similar to those of the broad magical tradition to be fully assimilated into it. I suspect not, however. Rather do I think it likely that the conceptual framework of Spare's occult system will always have a certain minority appeal and will continue to live alongside the main body of the tradition in a somewhat uneasy peaceful coexistence, probably in much the same way that Zen lives along with the more traditional Mahayana Buddhism.

[2] I cannot trace any published account of these new techniques—no doubt Mr. Kenneth Grant's long-awaited book on Spare will supply this want in due course—and I have had to rely on my friend's, possibly incorrect, memory of his conversation with Spare.

Additional Note There are today many admirers of A.O. Spare who practise what they term 'Chaos Magic'.

CHAPTER TWENTY-THREE

The Cubic Stone and Other New Organisations in the Golden Dawn Tradition

While it is true that during the twelve years 1939-1951 interest in oriental forms of occultism seems to have reached new heights there was a noticeable falling off in the numbers of those who wished to study and practice the western magical tradition. It is difficult to know exactly why this occurred, but I suspect that the horrid age of war, shortages, and austerity led occultists, as it did many other people, to desire a complete escape from their own intellectual and physical environment, and that this desire was more adequately fulfilled by Zen Buddhism and other exotic oriental cults than it was by the native tradition.

There seems to have been a mild revival of interest in Aleister Crowley after the publication of John Symond's biography of him in the autumn of 1951, and there was a sharp rise in the second-hand prices of the *Equinox* and other Crowleyana. It was not until about 1959 or 1960, however, that the Golden Dawn itself, rather than Crowley's derivation of it, began to attract the attention of a new generation of occultists.

These young would-be magicians were curiously different in personality and social background from their predecessors, for while the latter had been largely, although not entirely, middle-class in their origins, and usually right-wing, sometimes ex-

tremely right wing, in their politics,[1] the former were usually
red-brick graduates who had escaped from their working-class
backgrounds via the 1944 Education Act and the local Grammar School and were also predominantly left-wing in their
political attitudes—many of them had both demonstrated in
Trafalgar Square against Eden and his Suez adventure and had
marched the dusty roads from Aldermaston in the great days of
the Campaign for Nuclear Disarmament. Whilst the numbers
of these people must not be unduly exaggerated there were
enough of them to make the four volumes of Regardie's *Golden
Dawn*, the demand for which had been so small that it had
remained in print for twenty years, almost unobtainable by the
end of 1961—the few second-hand sets that came on to the
market fetched amazing prices, sometimes as much as eighty
pounds.

On the whole I do not think that these young occultists and
the groups and Orders that they have formed are very impressive. They seem more attracted to the mystery and glamour of
running a secret society, wearing impressive robes, claiming
exalted degrees etc. than they do to the idea of doing any
serious occult training and work. The Order that they have
founded and re-founded—for a series of schism, splits, quarrels
and re-unifications have caused the patterns of these organisations to change like those seen in a kaleidoscope—claim, without
any justification, to be 'the original Golden Dawn'[2] or 'older
than the Golden Dawn', but, on the whole, they are merely
fifth-rate imitations of that which they so unsuccessfully imitate.
The leaders of two of these groups are at odds, for each makes

[1] There were, of course, exceptions. The Stella Matutina included several
members of the Fabian Society in the ranks of its initiates, amongst them
Herbert Burrows and E. Nesbit (Mrs. Hubert Bland) the writer of children's
stories.

[2] Amusingly enough, when the A.O. material was found on a Sussex
beach (I have referred to this incident in my chapter entitled 'Regardie
and his Impact') members of no less than three of these groups approached
me with dramatic stories of how 'they were cut off by the tide while performing a magical ceremony and had to leave their equipment behind'.
These pretensions were given the lie by the fact that the material in
question was marked with the personal seal of Mrs. Tranchell-Hayes of the
A.O.

the claim that he is the re-incarnation of Aleister Crowley; I long to witness a meeting between the two, the clash between rival Beasts 666! It is not for me, mere mortal that I am, to say whether or not either of these claims is justified—but if one or other of these would-be Magi is Aleister Crowley returned to Earth, it must be admitted that since the end of his last incarnation in 1947 he has lost something like 99 per cent of his former literary, magical and verbal abilities.

There are, of course, exceptions to the general mediocrity, the most notable of them being the Order of the Cubic Stone, which operates in Wolverhampton and the Midlands. There are two important differences between the O.C.S. and most of the other contemporary magical groups; firstly, it makes no bogus claims to great antiquity, it frankly admits its compara-tively recent origin, and, secondly, its Chiefs are both competent and sincere—they have themselves done that which they teach.

The O.C.S. was founded in the mid 'sixties by an elderly occul-tist named Theodore Howard and two young scientific techni-cians named David Edwards and Robert Turner. Mr. Howard does not seem to have played much active part in running the Order and retired from his position after a comparatively short time, leaving the two younger occultists in control. Mr. Edwards and Mr. Turner arrived at the grades they claim by processes of self-initiation; the record of one such self-initiation was published in an issue of *The Monolith*, the Order's twice-yearly duplicated magazine. As this record, entitled *The Magical Ladder of Frater L.Z.I., the 4° = 7° to 5° = 6° Workings* contains many points of interest I think it worthwhile to reproduce some short extracts from it.

I open the Temple in the Grade of 1° = 10°. All went well until the Ritual of the Bornless One[3] when a hand, yellowish in colour, manifested on the left side of the Altar. It seemed to be the hand of a woman. It had no finger nails and was cut off at the wrist ... when my attention fully turned to-wards it, it dematerialised before my eyes. The Call of the

[3] A Golden Dawn ritual derived from a Graeco-Egyptian magical papyrus.

187

Thirtieth Aethyr[4] was successful, although it produced a condition in which I found it hard to breath.... The Call of the Lesser Angle produced a blast of air from the southern quarter of the Temple. This did not appear to be physical air as the candle ... burnt steadily without a flicker.

(Second Day) Open the Temple using the Zelator ritual.[5] Preliminary invocations produced a feeling of great peace and harmony ... noticed a blue haze in the East. Images strong throughout. Heard voices whispering to me throughout the Ritual of the Bornless One ... The Call of the 28th Aethyr produced the same effect as before only much worse. It was physical torment to draw breath.... At the commencement of the 7th Enochian Call a shower of bright yellow sparks burst from the candle which was burning on the right hand side of the altar....

(Third Day) Open the Temple by Practicus Ritual which lit the Temple up with a rose-coloured glow ... once more ... the impression of voices speaking to me. This time very low in pitch.... At the commencement of the Call of the Lesser Angle of Fire in the Element of Water[6] I was immediately aware of a presence in the circle to the right of the Altar....

(Fourth Day) I open the Temple in the Grade of Philosophus. The Binding of the Qlipoth[7] was followed by a great feeling of awareness due, I think, to the influx of power from the Solar Gods as I approach the Sphere of Tiphareth ... the Temple once more lit up in a rosy glow.... The invocation of Horus produced a feeling of dizzyness, my head spun, particularly at the phrase 'Strike, strike the master chord'.[8]

(Fifth Day) ... Open the Temple. Feeling of great devotion

[4] An aspect of the Enochian system of magic.

[5] In the O.C.S., as in Crowley's A.A., the grade of Zelator corresponds with the Element of Air and not, as in the Golden Dawn, with the Element of Earth.

[6] The reference is the 'Great Western Quadrangle of Water' in the Enochian system.

[7] The evil and averse Sephiroth of the Qabalistic Tree of Life, the spheres of unbalanced force.

[8] This is interesting, for it shows that the Invocation of Horus used was that devised by Crowley rather than some Golden Dawn ritual.

188

to the Great Work. Performed the Mass of the Phoenix facing the Western Quarter. Cut Qabalistic Cross upon breast with the white dagger of art; soaked up the blood with a cloth of white linen.[9] During the performance of the Firebird Rite the room became filled with mist and static sparks leapt and danced all over my body on giving the L.V.X. signs. I now understand the deep sacrificial significance of this rite.... Performing the Enochian Spirit Invocation ... the room took on a deep golden hue. I felt light-headed ... and for a few seconds I lost consciousness altogether. This condition cleared after opening the Portal of the Vault of the Adepti ... on Rending the Veil I felt that I had grown about two feet taller and things in the Temple diminished in size but became brighter and clearer. At the conclusion of the Sixth Might Aire[10] the floor of the Temple rocked violently for what seemed about ten seconds. After this I felt a presence within a circle near to the Eastern Watchtower. With this visitation came a feeling of peace and stability. I felt that I had been received into my rightful place. Even after performing the ... Banishing Rituals the presence was still with me, although the force field ensnared by my workings had been effectively dispersed.... I was sitting in quiet meditation, contemplating the work just completed when I sensed that the door (I had my back to it at the time) opened. I turned to look ... a thought picture very strong and clear welled up in my consciousness ... a middle aged man, very tall ... he may have been an Arabian. He stood before me and uttered a single word WAZROM.... Although WAZROM appeared ... fully formed, dark-skinned and robed in a heavy silken cloth of silver blue, the only part of his body that was visible was his head. There was nothing concealed where the arms should have been and the feet were concealed beneath his heavy and voluminous robe.

This then, I believe, was my Holy Guardian Angel.

[9] The Mass of the Phoenix is a specifically Thelemite (Crowleyan) ritual; a cross is quite literally cut on the breast, the idea being that freshly-shed blood liberates energy.

[10] Once again a reference to the Enochian system.

The duplicated leaflet that the O.C.S. sends to enquirers describes the aim of the Order as being to 'train the student in our approach to Ceremonial Magic in order that he may use this medium to obtain knowledge and to reach his goal'. The leaflet goes on to state that 'the system we use is based on the Qabalah and our teachings stem from the Golden Dawn and other similar sources'. To some extent the organisation now appears to be moving away from the Golden Dawn tradition, for in a recent interesting pamphlet entitled *Dare to Make Magic*, David Edwards, one of the Chiefs of the Order, stated that 'an Initiate ... should be capable of successfully performing any of the rituals classified by the Order of the Golden Dawn as being suitable for an Adeptus Minor. I am not specifically advocating these rituals as many of the Golden Dawn attributes and correspondences were completely erroneous'.[11]

The Monolith and the pamphlets issued by the group are usually of great interest. The quality of their English, however, is often markedly inferior to their content—sometimes, in fact, it verges on the semi-literate; I think that this is partly the result of extremely careless proof-reading, partly the result of the constitutional inability of most scientists to write a good, plain English sentence.

Perhaps the best summing up of the O.C.S. was made by a distinguished English ex-disciple of Crowley who said to me, (speaking about a lecture given by one of the Chiefs), 'Here are two young men, doing really first-class research on the Enochian system. Best of all, when they don't know something they are not afraid to say so.'

[11] Since writing the above passage Mr. Edwards has resigned from the Order, for what reason I do not know. The present Chiefs of the O.C.S. seem to be Mr. Turner and his wife.

Additional Note Throughout the 1980s many new magical Orders, influenced to a greater or lesser extent by Golden Dawn traditions, have been extremely active.

CHAPTER TWENTY-FOUR

A Summing Up

The revival of magic in the last eighty or ninety years is, at the very least, an odd phenomenon; at the best it is an encouraging indication that mankind will never cease its search for spiritual reality, will never be completely satisfied with the porcine requirements of a full trough and a warm sty. In this revival it is clear that the Golden Dawn and its derivatives were all-important; the inferiority of the organisations that evolved independently of the Golden Dawn, such as the Gardnerian witch-cult, is made apparent by simply reading their literature.

Much of the Golden Dawn system was not original, for component parts of it can be found scattered through the occult writings of a thousand years of European history. The achievement of Anna Sprengel (if she ever existed), Mathers, or his unknown occult teachers, was to synthesise a coherent, logical, system of practical occultism out of these scattered remains of a tradition that had been broken-up by fifteen hundred years of religious persecution.

In the last analysis it is quite unimportant whether the synthesiser was Mathers or someone else; the important thing is that those who have really worked at the system in all its aspects have found that it is effective, that it achieves what it sets out to achieve. No-one who has used the Golden Dawn system to evoke a 'spirit' from the dark realms of the Unconscious, to 'charge' a talisman, to attempt to travel astrally through the thirty Enochian 'Aires' from TEX to LIL can deny this effectiveness.

On the other hand, it cannot be denied that most members

of the original Order and, particularly, its later offshoots did not use the system effectively. Instead they got side-tracked into inflating their own egos by excessive astral travel and the futile search for 'hidden Masters'. Nevertheless, it would be a little early to say that Mathers and his early followers completely failed in that which they set out to achieve, for in the Bristol Hermanubis Temple and in one or two of the later offshoots, there is hope for the future of the tradition.

THE CIPHER MANUSCRIPTS' SKELETONIC FORM

Facing page 583 of A. E. Waite's *Brotherhood of the Rosy Cross* is a photograph of one page from the original cipher manuscript; for some mysterious reason this page is, in fact, printed upside down! A translation of this page is given below in order that the reader may appreciate that the manuscripts were not detailed rituals, but merely working notes, probably made by someone who had witnessed the ceremonies in a German Rosicrucian Temple. For reasons of clarity I have expanded the abbreviations given in manuscript into the words they represent.

Hierophant. No advance except by permit of second order.
In Hebrew—the ten sephiroth
exaltation—triplicities—letters and numbers
elements—zodiac signs—planets-houses
Hierophant tells subjects of necessary study
unbalanced is evil—persevere study equilibrium each be secret
never condemn others religion
to honour God as our light
Hiereus addressed neophyte and exhorts to memory
proclaims new neophyte
stolistes plus cup = cold—dadouchos plus censer = hot
with his wand and lamp
Kerux is a reconciler
Hegemon between pillars—white—mitre sceptre
Hiereus throne—robe—sword
note triad of life
path of occult science
of dead in them—between them is the Hegemon—pillars
   should have texts of ritual
a lamp on each
fixed and volatile
active and passive—severity and mercy

To illustrate the way in which Mathers transformed these notes I will take the lines 'never condemn others religion' and 'to honour God as our light'. The first became 'Remember that you hold all religions in reverence, for there is none but contains a ray from the ineffable Light that you are seeking' while the second became 'Remember that God alone is our Light and the Bestower of Perfect Wisdom, and that no mortal power can do more than bring you to the Pathway of that Wisdom, which He could, if it so pleased Him, put into the heart of a child. For as the whole is greater than the part, so are we but Sparks from the Insupportable Light which is in Him. The ends of the Earth are swept by the borders of His garment of flame, from Him all things proceed, and unto Him all things return. Therefore we invoke Him. Therefore even the Banner of the East falls in admiration before Him.'

APPENDIX B

MATHERS' VERSIONS OF THE GRIMOIRES

It was not until the nineteenth century that satisfactory printed editions of the Grimoires began to appear in English. At the beginning of the century a certain Francis Barrett gave classes on the Occult Sciences in Marylebone and it was he who published an ambitious work on Magic, Divination and Astrology in 1801. This book, *The Magus*, was a real attempt to separate the wheat of the genuine Theurgic tradition from the chaff that was thoroughly mixed with it in many of the Grimoires. While Barrett's labours were by no means completely successful and many of the formulae given were woefully incomplete and misleading it was a worthwhile effort and whole generations of occultists based their first tentative experiments in Ritual Magic and Ceremonial Skrying on information they extracted from *The Magus*. In the 'fifties and 'sixties of the nineteenth century a group of occultists experimenting with the techniques outlined in this work gathered round the mystic and visionary

Fred Hockley and by the 'seventies demand for *The Magus* was such that a London publisher found it worth while to reprint it. Later still an American Edition was published under the ridiculous title of *Hindu Magic* and it is interesting to note that a small edition of the book has recently been produced in England.

It was not, however, until Mathers gave the matter his attention that really satisfactory editions of the great classical Grimoires appeared. After he had completed the translations printed in his *Kaballah Unveiled*, Mathers decided to prepare a purified and definitive English text of the most widespread of all medieval magical texts the *Key of Solomon*. To this end he immersed himself in the British Museum's unrivalled collection of French, Italian and Latin versions of the 'Key' and eventually succeeded in restoring the corrupted Hebrew of the Names of Power and deleting certain techniques which copyists had inserted from such corrupt Black Magical texts as the 'Grimorium Verum'.

Mathers' edition of the *Key* is invaluable to the serious student of the classical methods of invocation and evocation and, while both the original edition and its 1909 reprint are almost impossible to obtain, a pirated American edition is still available although at rather a high price.

It is surprising to note that A. E. Waite believed that the *Key of Solomon* was a late Medieval forgery in spite of the fact that Josephus specifically referred to Jewish magical works attributed to Solomon. While Waite's view may have been tenable when he first put it forward in his *Book of Black Magic and Pacts* it is amazing that he still clung to it when he published his *Book of Ceremonial Magic*—for eight years previously a copy of the Hebrew original had been discovered in the library of a deceased Rabbi and a full description of it published by a Jewish scholar of considerable repute. In fact there seems little doubt that the *Key* as we have it is a slightly Christianised version of a Qabalistic magical system of considerable antiquity.

Mathers followed up his work on the Key by turning his attention to the *Lemegeton* or *Lesser Key of Solomon*. This book is divided into a preliminary definition of Magic, a brief introductory description of the entire opus and five (in some cases four) books. The content of these books is admirably described in the introduction:

> The First Part is a Book of Evil Spirits called Goetia, showing how Solomon bound up those spirits and used them in several things whereby he obtained great fame.
> The Second Part is a Book of Spirits, partly good and partly evil, which is called Theurgia-Goetia, or the Magical Wisdom of the Aerial Spirits.
> The Third Part is called the Pauline Art and treateth of the spirits allotted unto every degree of the 360 degrees of the Zodiac and also of the Signs, and the Hours.
> The Fourth Part is called the Art Almadel of Solomon and concerns those spirits which are set over the Quaternary of the Altitude.
> The Fifth Part is a Book of Orations and Prayers which Solomon did use upon the Altar in the Temple.

Only the first book of the *Lemegeton* has been printed in book form, the fourth book being printed in Ralph Shirley's *Occult Review* in 1915 and the other three books never having been printed at all. By 1898 Mathers had produced a satisfactory version of the First Book (the Goetia) which he lent to various members of the Golden Dawn. Copies were made of it and one of them came eventually to be owned by Alan Bennett who carried out a considerable amount of experimentation with the Goetic processes. When Bennett departed for Ceylon he gave his 'Goetia' to Crowley who, three years later, published it without Mathers' permission and in incomplete form. This pirate edition was in its turn pirated by an American publisher, and this pirate edition is still available, although it lacks Crowley's translation of paraphrases of the conjurations into the extraordinary Enochian or Angelic language which was revealed to the sixteenth century occultists Dee and Kelley and first printed in 1659 by Meric Casaubon in his *True Relation*. The Third, and by far the most important, Grimoire translated by Mathers was the *Sacred Magic of Abramelin the Mage*, first published in 1898 and reproduced by photo-lithography in

196

1956—once again there is also a pirated American edition. Mathers had first heard of the existence of the book from the Rev. A. F. A. Woodford, and some years later his attention was recalled to it by the writer Jules Bois, who was himself an initiate of the Parisian Ahathoor Temple of the Golden Dawn. Woodford had told Mathers that the description of the sage Mejnour in Bulwer Lytton's odd, now little read, but nevertheless fascinating novel *Zanoni* was based on that of Abramelin and it is true that there are odd resemblances between certain passages in Lytton's *Strange Story* and some of the descriptions in the Second Part of the Grimoire.

Whatever Lytton may or may not have known, one thing seems clear to me; in the system of Abramelin we have something which is of much greater importance and interest than anything contained in the rest of the Grimoires. In the second book we are given the bare bones of a synthetic structure that is for Western Ocultism what Bhakta and Mantra Yoga are for Indian Occultism.

An intense practical regimen lasting some six months is required and if this is satisfactorily completed it results in the aspirant gaining the 'Knowledge and Conversation of His Holy Guardian Angel' by which is meant, of course, not some external being but 'that in me which is more than me myself', the Divine Ground of our being which Bulwer Lytton called Adonai, the Golden Dawn called the Genius, and the older Theosophists called the Higher Self.

In his introduction Mathers sternly warned his readers against any use of the Magic Squares given in the book unless they had satisfactorily completed the preliminary operation. It may well, of course, be due to auto-suggestion but all those who have disregarded this advice seem to have got into difficulties; the following letter, published in the *Occult Review* of December 1929 is typical.

Desiring some information which I could not get in the ordinary way, I resorted to the System of Abramelin, and to this end prepared a copy of the necessary Talisman, perfecting it to the best of my ability with my little stock of knowledge. The ritual performed, I proceeded to clear my place of working. A little knowledge is a dangerous thing; my ritual was imperfect and I only rendered the Talisman useless without in any way impairing the activities of the entity invoked. This looks like nothing else than gross carelessness on my part; and to a certain extent this is true—but the point I wish to make is this, that my knowledge of this particular system, and therefore my ritual, were imperfect; and in any case, I had been shown no method of combating this particular entity when once aroused. Now note the results.

Unfortunately I have no account of the date when these occurrences began, but the first hint of trouble must have come on or about March 3rd, 1927. I can guess the date with fair accuracy because, as I was to learn, the manifestations were always strongest about the new moon, and after I had gone to sleep. Upon this occasion I can remember waking up suddenly with a vague feeling of terror oppressing me; yet it was no ordinary nightmare terror, but an imposed emotion that could be thrown off by an effort of the will. This passed almost as soon as I stood up, and I thought no more about it.

Again, on April 2nd, or thereabouts, I was troubled by the same feeling, but regarded it as nothing more than a severe nightmare, though the fact that my sleep was distorted towards the time of the new moon had occurred to me; while as full moon drew on, the nights were peaceful again.

The new moon of May 1st brought a recurrence of the trouble, this time very much more powerful, and necessitated an almost intolerable effort of will to cast it off. Also it was about this time that I first saw the entity which was rapidly obsessing me. It was not altogether unlovely to look at. The eyes were closed and it was bearded with long flowing hair. It seemed a blind force slowly waking to activity.

Now there are three points which I must make quite clear before I proceed. In the first place I was never attacked twice in the same night. Secondly, when I speak of physical happenings, the smashing of glass and voices, they were never, with one absolutely inexplicable exception, actual, but pure illusions; and this leads to the third point. Not one of these incidents happened while I was asleep. Always I found myself awake with the terror upon me and struggling violently to cast off the spell. I have had nightmares before, but no nightmare that I have ever had could hold my mind in its grip for minutes at a time as this thing did, or send me plunging through a ten foot high window to the ground below.

The first indication I had that these visitations were absolutely out of the ordinary course of events came on May 30th. About midnight I was suddenly awakened by a voice calling loudly, 'Look Out', and at once I became aware of a red serpent coiling and uncoiling itself under my bed, and reaching out onto the floor with its head. Just as it was about to attack me I jumped through my window, and came to earth among the rose bushes below, fortunately with no more damage than a badly bruised arm.

After this there was absolute peace until June 30th, when the real climax came. I had seen the thing again on the night of the new moon, and had noticed considerable changes in its appearance. Especially it seemed far more active, while its long hair had changed into serpent-heads. The night after I was awakened by a violent noise and jumped out of bed. I then saw the noise was caused by a great red obelisk which crashed through the west wall of my room, and leaned against the wall at the east end, smashing both that and the window to pieces but missing my bed, which was in an alcove to the left of its path. In its transit it had smashed all the mirrors, and the floor and top of my bed were strewn with broken glass and fragments of wood. This time the obsession must have lasted some minutes. I dared not move for fear of cutting myself, and to reach the matches—wherein, I knew, lay safety—I had to lean across the bed and again risk the glass. Yet in my heart I knew that all this was false, but had no power to move. I could only stand there, incapable, looking at the shattered room in a state of hopeless terror.

And now comes the most extraordinary part of the whole business. When I had finally mastered the obsession, I went to bed again dead tired, and I know that the only sound I made that night was jumping to the floor, also my room is at least a hundred yards from the rest of my family, yet next morning at breakfast I was asked what was the terrible noise in my room during the night.

After that I realised that the game was up. I had not taken these occurrences lying down, but I knew that it was impossible for me to control the force which I had set in motion. In desperation I turned to a good friend, who, I was aware, knew much of these things. She did not hesitate, but came at once to my assistance, and from that day to the present the trouble has absolutely gone from me.

APPENDIX C

THE ASTRAL WORKINGS OF THE SPHERE

The following are brief extracts from records of a series of experiments undertaken, in the summer of 1901, by members of Florence Farr's secret society, 'The Sphere'. The visions described by the Seer, a certain Soror I.O. of whose real identity I am uncertain, were intended to throw light on the nature of the Enochian alphabet. The meetings were held in the rooms of an Adeptus Minor called Humphreys who is also the 'I' of the record.

Sunday 21st July 1901. A vision of Sigillum AMTh in Temple in cave. Got a copy of marks on window in Valet Anchora Virtus' bedroom.

Monday 22nd July 1901. Vision continued but difficulties at first owing to hostile influences which I.O. said were due to the day being the anniversary of a suicide in my rooms. Vision of rows of columns leading to Temple and stated re worship five pointed star and of the four great symbols one was absent (? symbol of Tablet of Union) also stated that the Enochian letters referred to Intelligences as well as letters, and that the centre seemed not the North Pole but the Magnetic Pole.

Tuesday 23rd July 1901. In Chamber of Initiation are five

brethren. One speaks of the five Sigils of the Five Elements, Five Below and Five Above. There is an Altar sometimes transparent, sometimes opaque, under it is a luminosity from no visible source. The brethren had on yellow robes, with engraved band around waist, and the front ornament of each was an Eye. Round the neck the Enochian letters seemed woven into the garment. In their hands they held a curious Serpent twist(ing) up and back again upon itself. This seemed to have the power of giving transparency. I hear 'For All that is contains All'. The symbol on the Altar changes and instead of warmth there is now a rushing wind. The Altar, now no longer transparent, seems to float and ascend to blue space, and returns with yet another symbol. Altar and symbol seem effulgent. There is a light present—but beyond it there is sensation and harmony. Everything seems green. On handling symbol this turned to blue. An idea of a principle of force.

Now I am in a bare white chamber and I feel a sensation of great warmth, the white light seems to grow.

On the walls seem the double triangles which seem to grow and diminish on looking at them. Each of the points has its own Angel. The use of this symbol brings six powers.

July 24th, 1901. Scene, the original Chamber. The Magus directs the clairvoyant to take up position on Cross in Centre of Circle which is in turn in a square (? inverted Pentagon). This in turn in a Pentagram at each angle of which stands a figure: the walls recede.

At the North point which gives off a golden light is a winged figure, on his breast the Ankh. The clairvoyant drawn towards him (away from the centre). He seems the source of all vitality and more and of all light and more. In his hands he holds a Lotus which has seven leaves and a curved stem with only one leaf and that pointing towards the West. The Lotus half in shade suggesting day and night and more!

The Stamens seem to be a crown of gold. The petals seem to multiply as one looks. There are thirty of them. The petals are half white and half black and yet not black for a kind of blue permeates everything.

As I look the petals seem to expand and become globular and separate from the main stem and the spheres, part light and part dark, individualise and float away from east to west and dissolve.

The extraordinary thing about these records is that the Seer seems to have completely ignored the Golden Dawn techniques of astral vision; she seems to have been content to passively accept whatever pictures rose in her subconscious while she should have given the appropriate challenges, grade signs, banishing pentagrams etc.—if this had been done any false perceptions would have been revealed by, firstly, a marked fading of the colours seen and, secondly, a final disappearance of the illusion.

In a note on page 74 I have stated that Florence Farr had at one time been the mistress of W. B. Yeats. It has been suggested to me that this is intrinsically unlikely as, at the relevant period, Yeats was deeply emotionally involved with Maud Gonne. This latter involvement is a matter of history, but I see no reason to doubt the surviving Golden Dawn tradition that Yeats, for a time at least, had an active physical relationship with his fellow-initiate, although it was, I am sure, on a shallow emotional level.

The surviving Golden Dawn tradition is that Florence Farr was not a nymphomaniac—that she was not really greatly interested in sex—but that she was almost incapable of saying no to any man who asked her to sleep with him; I am satisfied that, on one occasion at least, she had physical intercourse with Aleister Crowley.

LATER TEACHING RECEIVED FROM MATHERS

Between 1908 and 1912 Mathers issued various side-lectures
and other manuscripts to those Temples that were loyal to him.
Much of this additional material reached the Stella Matutina
(via J. W. Brodie-Innes) but some did not do so and, consequently, is not included in Israel Regardie's edition of the Order
documents. Some of these later manuscripts are of great interest,
and one in particular, that seems to have been issued to Theorici
Adepti Minores, is of real importance; for it outlines an astrological system that differs in some respects from both the normal
western astrology (taught, in the Golden Dawn and its offshoots,
to members of the Portal Grade) and the sidereal ('starry') astrology used by the Hindus and a minority of modern western
astrologers.

In considering this 'initiated astrology' it must be borne in
mind that the signs of the zodiac in popular astrology are
completely out of step with the constellations bearing the same
names. This situation has arisen because of the precession of
the equinox—the fact that the equinoctial point (i.e. the point
of the zodiac at which the sun lies when it crosses the equator
on March 21st each year) moves steadily through the zodiac in
a reverse direction to the motion of the planets. In spite of this
fact exoteric astrologers insist on calling this invisible, moving
equinoctial point the 0° of Aries although it is, in reality, many
degrees away from the constellation of that name.

In Mathers' system the moving, or tropical, zodiac is abandoned in favour of a fixed sidereal zodiac in which the signs
and constellations coincide and is measured from the star called
Regulus, which is taken as being in 0° Leo. This sidereal zodiac
requires a correction to the tropical longitudes given in all
ephemerides (lists of planetary and zodiacal positions) used by
astrologers—and this correction varies each year. Mathers supplied a table of these corrections for the years 1800-1911; as it
seems likely that some of the readers of this book will have
astrological interests—a recent poll showed that no less than

twenty per cent of the adult population of England and Wales take astrology seriously—I think it worth reproduction; in each case Column I indicates the year and Column II indicates the degrees and minutes to be subtracted from the planetary and house positions as calculated from an ephemeris.

Col I	Col II	Col I	Col II	Col I	Col II	Col I	Col II
1800	27 4	1828	27 27	1856	27 51	1884	28 13
1801	27 5	1829	27 28	1857	27 52	1885	28 14
1802	27 6	1830	27 29	1858	27 53	1886	28 15
1803	27 7	1831	27 30	1859	27 53	1887	28 15
1804	27 8	1832	27 31	1860	27 54	1888	28 16
1805	27 8	1833	27 31	1861	27 55	1889	28 17
1806	27 9	1834	27 32	1862	27 56	1890	28 18
1807	27 10	1835	27 33	1863	27 56	1891	28 19
1808	27 11	1836	27 34	1864	27 57	1892	28 20
1809	27 12	1837	27 35	1865	27 58	1893	28 21
1810	27 12	1838	27 35	1866	27 59	1894	28 22
1811	27 13	1839	27 37	1867	27 59	1895	28 23
1812	27 14	1840	27 37	1868	28 0	1896	28 24
1813	27 15	1841	27 38	1869	28 01	1897	28 25
1814	27 16	1842	27 39	1870	28 01	1898	28 26
1815	27 17	1843	27 40	1871	28 02	1899	28 27
1816	27 18	1844	27 41	1872	28 03	1900	28 28
1817	27 19	1845	27 42	1873	28 04	1901	28 29
1818	27 19	1846	27 43	1874	28 05	1902	28 30
1819	27 20	1847	27 44	1875	28 06	1803	28 31
1820	27 21	1848	27 44	1876	28 06	1904	28 32
1821	27 22	1849	27 45	1877	28 07	1905	28 32
1822	27 23	1850	27 46	1878	28 08	1906	28 33
1823	27 23	1851	27 47	1879	28 09	1907	28 34
1824	27 24	1852	27 48	1880	28 10	1908	28 35
1825	27 25	1853	27 49	1881	28 11	1909	28 36
1826	27 26	1854	27 50	1882	28 11	1910	28 37
1827	27 27	1855	27 50	1883	28 12	1911	28 37

I am not myself an astrologer, but a friend who does practice that art tells me that applying these corrections to the charts of well-known figures often produces meaningful and helpful amendments. One example he gives is that of the horoscope of King George VI. He writes:

> In the exoterically calculated nativity of King George VI no planet is either in its exaltation or dignity, but if the whole thing is redone according to the G.D. system both Venus and Mars are brought into the signs of their dignity, as one would expect in a happily-married monarch who was also commander-in-chief of his armed forces. In view of certain events in the late King's life it is also significant that his Ascendant changes from Libra to Virgo.

It is also interesting to note that on the Mathers system we enter the so-called 'Aquarian Age' in about 2010 A.D. and not, as most occultists teach, something like three hundred years later.

The house division system used in this Golden Dawn astrology was neither that of Placidus, used by almost all nineteenth-century astrologers, nor the 'equal' system used by many contemporary astrologers. Instead, the ascendant, I-C, Descendant, and M.C. were the boundaries of the first, fourth, seventh, and tenth houses and each of the four segments was then divided into three equal houses.

APPENDIX E

THE IDENTITY OF STEINER'S TEACHERS

Those who have considered the matter, have always found it surprising that, until he reached the age of forty, Rudolf Steiner appears to have had little or no interest in, or contact with, the esoteric tradition or organised occult bodies, while from 1902 until the date of his death in 1925, he produced an astonishing series of books, pamphlets, articles, and lectures on almost every aspect of occultism from the history of Atlantis to the nature and significance of the human blood.

For over fifty years Steiner's followers in the Anthroposophical Society have claimed that their master's teachings were the product of his own unaided clairvoyance and self-initiation, and of them alone. To many of those who have read Steiner, myself among them, this has always seemed inherently improbable. In the chapter of this book entitled 'Dr. Felkin seeks a Master' I have given some account of the German Temples under Steiner's control and indicated my reasons for believing that they were in some way connected with the Ordo Templi Orientis.

A communication which I have received from a German occultist who wishes to remain anonymous goes into some detail about Steiner's Rosicrucian and Templar connections. While this communication must be treated with some reserve, as it is not backed up by any documentation, to me it has the ring of truth and I therefore think that parts of it are worthy of reproduction.[1]

Steiner joined the occult-masonic rite led by Klein and Hartmann in 1902. At first they treated him with great reserve, for they thought him as not genuine but an academic striving for fame by writing about masons for Karl Kautsky[2] and his papers so that he might get into the positions of power. Later they decided that this was not so and initiated him into the Brothers of Light and the Rosicrucian Illuminati[3] who were real occultists and not the revolutionary and political Illuminati of Weishaupt.

In 1905 Steiner was chartered to have a lodge of the Eastern Templars.[4] Steiner sometimes called his lodge 'Secret Masonry' for the first three degrees were the same almost as those of the ordinary masons.[5] He worked with Reuss until 1914 but their world-picture-philosophy was not the same for Steiner did

---

[1] I have ventured to correct the English where it verged upon the incomprehensible, otherwise I reproduce these extracts in the form they were received.
[2] A German socialist leader of the period.
[3] This puzzles me; I have always understood that the German attempt to revive the Illuminati was unsuccessful.
[4] This, clearly, can be nothing but the O.T.O.
[5] This is extremely significant, for in 1917 Crowley rewrote the first three degrees of the O.T.O. because American freemasons had complained that they were too similar to their own degrees.

not use the physical sex but only the stored-up Kundalini serpent sex (the white sex magic). So his high degrees saw the symbols in a different way.

Steiner was a natural clairvoyant but only could this be released when Klein initiated him and opened the pineal gland and other centres. Then he saw everything in the Akasha.

Steiner did not like Reuss and would not use his new rite or new Mass in 1914. Many other Templars also thought Reuss had become very black. But they also did not like Steiner because he came under astral influence hostile to Germany and thus made von Moltke lose the big invasion battle in France. Steiner did not use masonic rites after 1917.

APPENDIX F

THE CROMLECH TEMPLE'S TEACHINGS ON MORALITY AND SEXUALITY

The Temple's teachings on these subjects are given in its so-called Aura E 3 papers; extracts from these are as follows:

Among human beings, the concourse of male and female is everywhere, and has been in every age controlled by marriage laws and customs, which vary greatly in different races, but often are stronger than the very precepts of their faiths, and often appear to that race to be so self evident that they cannot imagine any other custom being other than very evil, and their most earnest desire is to impose their own marriage customs on all the world.

Accompanying this there is, in the vast majority of human beings, especially in the West, and especially in modern times, a reliance, an instinctive secrecy, in all concerning the act of sex, so instinctive that it appears natural and inevitable. Universally, then, we find the sex-functions set apart in a separate category, by the precepts of every faith, and by universal instinct, an inner shrine as it were, a thing forbid, save on definite conditions, and those always of privacy. The guards which have always been set around these functions have collectively been called the 'Great Taboo'....

It would be difficult for a materialistic and utilitarian philosopher, such as Jeremy Bentham for instance, approaching the subject entirely without preconception, to find any rational cause for the Great Taboo. The bodily functions of eating, drinking, assimilation and nutrition are essential to continuance of the species but are subject to no taboo, except among a few tribes of (so-called) primitive man. Why then should the function of reproduction be subject thereto, and that only among mankind? For the Taboo if it exists at all among animals is very rare. Yet it is undoubtedly so strong that the conclusion is inevitable that it depends on some essential element in the Aura.

... we find that the Aura is of the nature of a magnetic field, and such magnetic fields can arise only from the duel polarity of the magnet. We expect, then, to find this quality of dual polarity—two contending forces—manifest in the Aura.

The quality of sex attraction is, we know, of enormous, often of irresistible, force—and, against this, the other contending force is the Great Taboo. These two forces are manifested in every sane Aura, and in varying degrees and proportions. In the ordinary and unitiated mass of mankind ... the counteraction of these two forces ... produces the morality of the race and time. And as the proportion and intensity varies, so does the natural and instinctive morality.

Thus, taking the very simplest case, while in the normal and healthy human being the sex attraction is the strongest of all motives of action, every faith in the world imposes on the attraction the conditions of some form of marriage, and custom, which has through the ages become so inevitable as to be an instinct, imposes also the condition of privacy in its performance, and thus the Taboo governs and restrains the natural force, and the resultant tends to enable the control of the body by the spirit. These restrictions are exceedingly various ... some form of restriction is universal and ... its origin is in the operation of the Great Taboo on the typical

Aura of the particular race and time, and this causes that form of restriction to be generally accepted and enforced.

Thus to the ordinary Western of our time, it would be useless to bring arguments, either social or religious in favour of polygamy, and to many Easterns arguments in favour of monogamy would seem absurd. The Adept notes the typical Aura and concludes that that particular manifestation of the Great Taboo, and that particular proportion between its strength and that of the sex attraction, produces exactly the natural and instinctive morality ... needed at that time and place. But we find also in every human being and also in the collective Aura of every nation or tribe, a tendency to rebel against the Taboo—a desire to violate it in some point —and that not only merely by the superior force of the sex attraction, but often as a philosophic theorem, by those who never themselves violate, or wish to violate its rules. Thus the Taboo itself is kept in a continual state of flux.

Now the Exempt Adept ... assumes that these two forces being both implanted by God, are both in accordance with His will, and that their manifestation and proportion varying as we have seen, there can be no hard and fast ratio which is His will and all others vile and sinful ... and he tries to discover the meaning of the variations and whereto each tends.

Moreover, recognising that the Taboo itself belongs to the Aura of which it is a natural characteristic, he can detach his consciousness therefrom, and enquire with no need for reticence or prejudice or preconception, what is the meaning and symbology of the act of sex, what its results beyond those known to the outer and uninitiated. In other words, he can pass beyond the Taboo, and so can see why the Taboo has been made by God's providence as an essential part of man's Aura.

... the ratio between the Sex-Attraction and the Great Taboo indicates the ordinary average morality of the race or time. But occasionally we find that this ratio varies enormously in different individuals of the same race and period. Thus in Medieval Italy the sex attraction among the nobles was enormously strong, and very slightly restrained by the Taboo. The precepts of Religion were the same then as now, but had very slight effect, the instincts of reticence were also comparatively slight.

In the romances, the philosophical discourses, the pictures and the cartoons, the sex-relations were freely and openly dealt with. But by reaction from this, we find a large class with whom the Taboo was extraordinarily powerful—the Ascetics refusing to allow even the least approval to the natural sex-attraction. The whole force of the Taboo being directed, not to regulate, but entirely to inhibit and destroy that attraction, it thus became regarded by them as a thing of evil in itself, however much controlled or restrained. The average ratio of the two forces remained practically normal but was abnormal in individuals. And we find that in this race and period the mass of people, who were neither licentious nobles nor Ascetics, had a normal morality of religion and custom. We have to recognise, therefore, that either of these two forces may be abnormally developed, and the balance may be lost. And in this loss of equilibrium, if it be permanent and excessive, is insanity.

Both types of insanity are well known, the sex maniac who is under no restraint, for whom the Taboo does not exist, and the Ascetic fanatic, who kills out every sexual desire or possibility, who even has been known to consider self-castration an acceptable offering to God.

But these types are valuable studies ... as showing one of the dual forces isolated and operating unrestrained.

We have only now to notice that, of the dual forces, the sex-attraction has its origin in the body itself, the symbols in the Aura being formed and vivified from within, by the magnetism generated by the body itself.

The Great Taboo restraining the sex instinct comes from without, and is infused in the Aura by supernatural forces. Hence the commonly received idea that the attraction is material and therefore naturally base and evil, the Taboo ... is divine and imposed by God. The Adept, however, must recognise that the body with all its functions is God's own creation, and the dual polarity, the force and the restraint, is the divine formula of all creation, from the flower to the man.

... the Adamic aspect of the Taboo ... does not always operate even in the race of Adam—whence it happens that there are some to whom sometimes what under the Taboo is called obscene and unclean, or at best indelicate, seems the highest good of all. Careful examination by Exempt Adepts indicates that in these cases there is a temporary shutting off of certain magnetic currents in that pole whence arises the forces of the Taboo. Those in whom these forces are acting strongly are usually intense in their scorn and reprobation. Whence the man or woman in whose Aura for a time (usually short) those forces cease to function, carefully conceals his or her actions, lest they should be a cause of offence to others. It is such a modification of the forces of Taboo that often takes a man to the society of prostitutes. Some speak of what they term a filthy delight in indecency. But it is, in fact, the normal nature of humanity for the moment freed from restraint.

We must recognise that both the freeing and the restraint are the purpose of the Ruler of the Universe, and from these characteristics is the power to advance drawn. Neither, in fact, is good or ill. But the reprobation of those who are under the Taboo is part of the scheme and an essential element in the Taboo. The exempt Adept does not share it. So far as his, he modifies its acerbity as did the Master—'He that is without sin let him cast the first stone.'

Those who are still under the Taboo will say of those thus temporarily freed, that they are coarse, brutal, animal creatures without refinement.

But the knowledge of mankind denies this in toto. For we know well that men of high intellect, of brilliant artistic capacity and great spirituality have periods when they must needs defy all the conventions of morality, reserve, and what is called decency; and that not, as is often stated as a reaction, but as part of the nature, kept normally veiled, but occasionally manifesting. Also refined and delicately nurtured women sometimes manifest similar qualities, though, in their case, under still subtler veils of secrecy. These men and women we find to be usually of considerable power and influence.

But those of the type called pure some fifty years ago, to whom sex was a thing reluctantly tolerated, never spoken of, and hardly known, rarely achieved any power or made any mark in the world. Though here we must note that there are other qualities than those of sex, governed by other restraints than the Taboo, where from also powerful currents may be generated. (For example the forces of Mars ...).

APPENDIX G

THE GOLDEN DAWN'S OFFICIAL HISTORY LECTURE

This History Lecture was delivered, and almost certainly written, by Wynn Westcott. I have heard it confidently stated that it dates from 1888 but as it refers to the death of Madame Blavatsky it cannot have been written before May 8th, 1891.[1] This document is not included in Regardie's edition of the Order Lectures and Rituals although in the early Temples it was issued to all newly initiated Neophytes.

The Order of the G.D. in the Outer is an Hermetic Society whose members are taught the principles of Occult Science and the Magic of Hermes.

During the early part of the second half of this century several eminent Adepts and Chiefs of this Order in France and England died, and their deaths caused a temporary dormant condition of Temple work. Prominent among the Adepts of our Order, and of public renown were Eliphas Levi the greatest of modern Magi; Ragon the author of several classical

---

[1] In view of its reference to the 'Library of the Second Order' the document probably dates from after 1892—but this is not necessarily so, for the phrase may simply refer to the private library of Mathers and Westcott. On the other hand, it cannot be later than 1894 because it excludes Ahathoor No. 7, which was consecrated that year, from its list of Temples.

books of occult lore; Kenneth R. H. MacKenzie the author of the famous and learned Masonic Encyclopaedia; and Frederick Hockley, possessed of the power of vision in crystal, and whose M.S.S. are highly esteemed.

These and other contemporary Adepti of this Order received their knowledge and power from predecessors of equal and even of greater eminence, they received indeed and have handed down to us this Doctrine and System of Theosophy and Hermetic Science, and the Higher Alchemy from a long series of practical investigators, whose origin is traced to the Fratres Rosae Crucis of Germany, which association was founded by one Christian Rosenkreutz about the year 1398.

The renowned German mystic and theologian Valentine Andreae has left us, in his works published about the year 1614, an account and exoteric arrangement of this Rosicrucian Society: it seems likely that it was Andreae who edited and published in 1614 the *Fama Fraternitatis* or *History of the Society* which must have been derived from the old records of the immediate pupils of C.R.

But even the Rosicrucian revival of mysticism was but a new development of the vastly older wisdom of the Qabalistic Rabbis, and of that very ancient secret knowledge, the Magic of the Egyptians in which the Hebrew Pentateuch tells you that Moses, the founder of the Jewish System was 'learned', that is, in which he had been initiated.

Through the Hebrew Qabalah indeed Europe became possessed of more of the ancient wisdom, than from any other one source, for it must be borne in mind that the Hebrews were taught at one time by the Egyptians and at a later date by the Chaldee Sages of Babylon.

It is a very curious fact that the so-called classic nations, the Greeks and the Romans, have handed down to us but slight glimpses of the Ancient Magic: and this is the more notable because Greece succeeded to the mastership of Egypt, and Rome to the Empire both of the Greeks and of the Jews.

Greece did indeed succeed to a share in the mysteries of the Egyptians, for the Eleusinian Mysteries were copies of those more ancient and solemn ceremonies of Isis, Osiris, and Seraphis; but they lacked the true Magic of Egypt, and further the classic writings retain but faint glimpses of even the Eleusinian Mysteries.

These glimpses serve also, be it noticed, to disclose the fact that the Eleusinian pupils were partly ignorant of the true Isiac Mysteries, a notable example of which is seen in the use of the words KONX OM PAX of which even they knew not the meaning: the words being the Greek imitation or translation of really ancient Egyptian words whose meaning has been kept secret for centuries.

Hence the 0° = 0° Grade of Neophyte is found to possess Egyptian characteristics and symbolism and further an attentive study of the Higher Grades will reveal the source of much of the culture and illustrate the language of the late Eliphas Levi, through whose Adeptship and advocacy the study of occultism has been popularised.

The first Order is a group of Four Grades, to each of which in succession Neophytes are admissable when duly approved by the Greatly Honoured Chiefs, after showing themselves possessed of sufficient aptitude and knowledge.

Beyond the above there are Three Grades of Adeptship, forming the Second Order, these have the power of selecting candidates, initiating students into the lowest Grades, and their Chiefs have in addition the power of issuing warrants of Temples, such as that of Isis Urania.

But the highest of all in this ancient scheme are the great Rulers of the whole System who severally sustain and govern the Third Order, which includes Three Magic Titles of Honour and Supremacy. These represent the Supernal Triad of the Sephiroth and are shrouded and unapproachable to the profane and to all other but the Chiefs of the Adepts: in case of a vacancy in this Order the Chief, most learned and most famous Adept obtains by decree the well earned record.

The Scheme of the G.D. then is formed upon the type of the Decad of the Sephiroth, the Ten Emanations of Deity as figures in the very ancient Qabalah of the Hebrews, whose professors were illuminated by the Higher Magic of the ancient world. The grades of the First Order will be found to be of

Hebrew design and tendency: and in as much as the efflux of time brought on the revelation of the Christos, the Tiphereth, the Beauty of the Microprosopus, Christian design is reflected in the Higher degrees.

The Neophyte Grade and the 1st, 2nd, 3rd, and 4th grades which this present Isis Urania Temple is authorised to confer, after due examination and approval in each case, possess Rituals and Secrets which have been received from the Greatly Honoured Chief Adepts, and these are placed in our hands to use in the tuition of pupils in the ancient methods of the Order.

This Temple was consecrated as a successor to Hermanubis No 2 which had ceased to exist owing to the decease of all its Chiefs.[2]

The Temple No. 1 of 'Licht, Liebe, Leben' is a group of Continental Mystics who have not been in the habit of performing ceremonies in open Lodge but have conferred the grades chiefly in privacy and in the presence of two or three members: for this reason there is no accurate record of the name and rank of all their members, and very great reticence is shown by them in their communications.

Very soon after the formation of this Temple No. 3, permission was granted for the consecration of Osiris Temple No. 4 at Weston-super-Mare under the rule of our very Honoured Frater Crux dat Salutem and the West of England has been assigned to him as a province. Almost at the same time the Horus Temple No. 5, under the rule of Very Honoured Frater Voto Vita Mea was also consecrated at Bradford in Yorkshire. These three Temples have members not only in this country, but in the United States, Hindostan, Palestine, Denmark, etc.

It will be convenient if I now give you the name of our Order in the several languages.

In the Hebrew the title is Chalbrath or Cheurah Lereh sour bokher, which means Society of the Shining Light of the Dawn. While yet Latin was the language in almost universal use amongst persons of culture, the name was Aurora. In

[2] The actual identity of 'Hermanubis' No. 2 is a complete mystery to me. I have heard it suggested that this was a Temple headed by Mackenzie and Hockley, but I think it far more likely that it was a German Temple.

Greek Heleos ehruse. In French L'Aube dorée. In German the title is Die Goldene Dämmerung.

Reference may be made to the Rosicrucian Society which was reconstructed by Frater Robert Wentworth Little, a student of the Mysteries. This Society, which has branches in England, Scotland and the United States, is allied to the G.D. It perpetuates one form of Rosicrucian initiation which was conferred a hundred years ago in England, and which is mentioned by Godfrey Higgins in his famous work *The Anacalypsis* or an attempt to withdraw the Veil of the Saitic Isis. Frater Little was a student of the school of Levi, and was also an eminent Freemason—and the Rosicrucian Society as revived by him, was made by intention and permission, essentially Masonic, thus severing all connection with those many Adepts who have not been 'Craftsmen', of whom history relates to us the splendid mental achievements, as of Basil Valentine, Artephius, Nicholas Flamel, Petrus of Abano, Cardan, Gafarelli, Jacob Boehme and Robert Fludd. The Rosicrucian Society in the same manner fails to recognise any worth for occult research in Woman. This is also an innovation upon the scheme of the ancient mysteries, in many of which, notably those of Isis, priestesses and Virgin prophetesses were prominent ministers. I wish indeed to call especial attention to the fact that in several instances in the ancient M.S.S. of our Order, which are written in cypher—where reference is made to the fratres and sorores, the words 'her or him' occur, thus clearly showing that in olden time, as at the present day, women rose to high rank and attainments in the secret Knowledge of the Order. History is by no means silent in respect to the success of women in occult researches, mention may suitably be made of Pernelle the wife and fellow worker of Nicholas Flamel: of Martine Bethereau, companion of the Baron Jean de Chatelet, who died about 1645, and of the widow lady (afterwards symbolised by him as Sophia, heavenly Wisdom) fellow student and inspirer of Johann Georg Gichtel who died in 1700 famous as a mystic Theosophist. The Occultist of today cannot need to be reminded of the great Hermetists and Theosophists of recent times, of Dr. Anna Kingsford of whom death prematurely robbed us, she was indeed illuminated by the Sun of Light and no one who ever heard her lectures and discuss the Hermetic Doctrines will ever forget her learning or her eloquence, her beauty or her grace.

Of Madame Blavatsky still more recently deceased, the leader of the Theosophical Society and teacher of Indian Esoteric Theosophy, no occult student, however wide apart may be his or her own favoured path to wisdom, could fail to recognise in her a master mind in a woman's frame.

While speaking to you of the losses which Occultism has recently suffered by the hand of death, I cannot fail to express to you the lament which followed the passing away of our dear friend Dr. Wm. Robert Woodman, for many years an officer of this Temple and a high Adeptus of the Second Order. He was a facile Hebrew scholar and an accomplished Qabalist: many of his MSS are in the Library of the Second Order: and in losing him from among us we all felt we had lost a pillar of Strength and of Benevolence. He was for many years known to the public as the Supreme Magus of the Soc Ros in Anglia which is exoteric in its outer grades, but its concerns are regulated by an Inner Circle of Adepts, who still hold the secrets of the R.C. and the private information of the Masonic Society.

The Eastern School of Theosophy and Occultism and our own Hermetic Society of the G.D. are fraternities of Students whose predecessors must have come from the same stock of Magi—the Scientific Priests of a remote antiquity. The two Societies differing in mode of teaching, and in language, are allied by mutual understanding and respect and their aim is similar.

Be well assured, my Frater, that the Order of the G.D., of which you have now become a member, can show you the way to much secret Knowledge, and to much Spiritual progress: it can, we believe, lead true and patient students who can Will, Dare, Learn and be Silent to the Summum Bonum, True Wisdom and Perfect Happiness.

SELECTED BIBLIOGRAPHY AND A NOTE ON SOURCES

I feel it advisable to preface my bibliography with a note indicating both (a) the printed books I have found most useful and (b) the sources on which I have most heavily relied.

Among the major source books of anyone who wishes to examine the nature of ritual magic in its modern versions must be F. Israel Regardie's *Golden Dawn*—his edition of the rituals and instructional lectures of that Order, or, to be more correct, the Stella Matutina versions of these rituals.[1] The same author's *My Rosicrucian Adventure* gives a most interesting, although perhaps slightly one-sided, account of the internal organisation of the Stella Matutina in the period 1934-36; the historical parts of that work, however, are extremely brief and rather inaccurate.

Also extremely valuable are A. E. Waite's autobiography *Shadows of Life and Thought*, although the relevant dates are given incorrectly and certain passages were, in my opinion, written with the deliberate object of deceiving the reader, and Mrs. Stoddart's series of articles in *The Patriot*. These articles, in spite of their ravings about alleged German-Jewish plots to take over the world, give a great deal of information about the Stella Matutina in the period 1903-1919. I have been able to check about 50 per cent of her quotations with original manuscripts now owned by the Bristol Hermanubis Temple and in every case I have found them accurate, although in many cases she has interjected her own comments into the middle of the quotations in question.

For my account of the revolt of the Second Order against Mathers I have relied on unpublished letters, documents, and pamphlets supplemented by the account given by J. F. C. Fuller in Vol. I No. 3 of the *Equinox*. For the story of the events lead-

---

[1] In fact the versions given by Regardie show very little variation from pre-1903 manuscript material. It is to be presumed that Dr. Regardie used the oldest copies he could trace.

ing to the departure of W. B. Yeats and Annie Horniman from the Order I have likewise relied on internal material.

There are no printed references to the Cromlech Temple or the Bristol Hermanubis Temple; I have used manuscripts and private communications from Fratres L. de L. and C.C.; these two, now elderly, occultists have also been immensely helpful to me in indicating the most reliable of two or more conflicting accounts of the same event.

For my accounts of Crowley's A.A. and O.T.O. I am particularly indebted to two former members of these organisations. For those interested in a detailed account of how Crowley trained his pupils in the years 1909-14 I would recommend Miss Jean Overton Fuller's fascinating *The Magical Dilemma of Victor B. Neuburg*. Her chapter on the Golden Dawn, however, is marred by a number of inaccuracies—for example, she attributes Wynn Westcott's motto of 'Sapere Aude' to someone else and confuses the grade-structure of the Golden Dawn with that of Crowley's Order.

There are no really satisfactory works in English dealing with either the Rosicrucians or the general background of nineteenth-century occultism. The voluminous works of A. E. Waite I have found helpful; they should be cautiously used, however, for, in spite of the scholarship on which he prided himself, their author often drifted into inaccurate generalisation.

Finally, I wish to refer to a book not yet finished; in the early part of 1970, when my own book was almost finished, I made the acquaintance of Mr. Ellic Howe who was engaged in writing *The Magicians*, which may be completed in 1971. Mr. Howe will deal with the period 1865-1900 in greater depth, and I have no doubt that his knowledge of obscure German sources will add to my knowledge of such interesting characters as Karl Kellner. At first we thought our books would be rivals, but over many friendly, and often hilarious, conversations we came to the conclusion that they would complement one another.

BIBLIOGRAPHY

ACHAD, FRATER (i.e. C. S. JONES). *Chalice of Ecstacy.* Yogi Publication Society, Chicago, 1923.

Q.B.L. or the Bride's Reception. Privately Printed, Chicago, 1923.

Anatomy of the Body of God. Privately Printed, Chicago, 1925.

XXXI Hymns to the Star Goddess. Will Ransom, 1923.

Crystal Vision through Crystal Gazing. Yogi Publication Society, 1923.

De Mysteriis R.R. et A.C. North American Publishing Co., 1924.

Liber Q.N.A. Unpublished, *circa* 1936.

Official Correspondence Concerning MA-ION. Unpublished, 1947-8.

ANON. *Manifesto of British Section O.T.O.* Privately printed.

ANON. *Manifesto of New Isis Lodge.* Privately printed.

BATHURST, L. (i.e. LEILA WADDELL). *Manifesto of M.M.M.* London, *circa* 1913.

CLYMER, R. S. *Rosicrucian Fraternities in America.* P.P. Co., 1930-35.

CROWLEY, ALEISTER. *Equinox* Vol. I, Nos. 1-10. London, 1909-13.

Equinox Vol. III, No. 1. Detroit, 1919.

Revival of Magick. Articles published New York, 1918.

CROW, W. B. *History of Magic, Witchcraft, and Occultism.* Aquarian Press, 1968.

CULLING, L. *Complete Magick Curriculum.* Llewellyn, 1969.

FORTUNE, DION (i.e. VIOLET EVANS). *Psychic Self Defence.* Rider, 1930.

Ceremonial Magic Unveiled. Occult Review, Jan. 1933.

FULLER, JEAN OVERTON. *Magical Dilemma of Victor Neuburg.* W. H. Allen, 1965.

GARDNER, G. B. *Meaning of Witchcraft.* Rider, 1954.

LEVI, ELIPHAS (i.e. A. L. CONSTANT). *Dogma of High Magic. Ritual of High Magic. History of Magic. Key of the Mysteries.* Paris 1854-61. Rider publish good English translations.

BIBLIOGRAPHY

MATHERS, S. L. MACGREGOR. *Kabbalah Unveiled*. Routledge and
  Kegan Paul.
  Greater Key of Solomon. Redway, 1888.
  Sacred Magic of Abramelin. Watkins, 1898.
REGARDIE, FRANCIS ISRAEL. *My Rosicrucian Adventure*. Aries
  Press. 1936.
  Golden Dawn. 4 vols. Aries Press, 1937-40.[1]
  Tree of Life. Rider, 1932.[2]
  Garden of Pomegranates. Rider, 1932.
WAITE, A. E. *Studies in Mysticism*. Hodder and Stoughton, 1906.
  Shadows of Life and Thought. Selwyn and Blount, 1938.
  Real History of the Rosicrucians. Redway, 1888.
YEATS, W. B. *Is the R.R. et A.C. to remain a Real Magical Order?*
  Privately Printed, 1901.
  Autobiographies. Macmillan, 1926.

[1] Reissued 1969 with new introductions and distributed by Llewellyn
Publishing Co., Minnesota.
[2] Reissued 1969 by Samuel L. Weiser of New York.

RECOMMENDED ADDITIONAL READING

Cavendish, Richard *The Magical Arts* Arkana, 1984
d'Arch Smith, Timothy *The Books of the Beast* Crucible, 1987
Gilbert, R.A. (editor) *The Sorcerer and His Apprentice* Aquarian,
  1983
King, Francis X *The Magical World of Aleister Crowley* Arrow,
  1987
Mathers, S.L. MacGregor *Astral Projection, Ritual Magic and
  Alchemy* Aquarian, 1987
Regardie, Israel *Complete Golden Dawn System of Magic* Falcon,
  1984
Richardson, Alan *Priestess* Aquarian, 1987
Skinner, Stephen *The Oracle of Geomancy* Prism, 1986
Suster, Gerald *Legacy of the Beast* W.H. Allen, 1988

INDEX[1]

[1] The names of leading personalities are followed by their Order mottoes—the so-called magical names.